When we come up against fear a  have the truth of God's Word as bat it. In *Fierce Faith*, Alli not onl Christ we are already victorious she also provides practical steps that will equip us to take hold of that promise and activate it in our own lives.

CHRISTINE CAINE, Founder of A21 and Propel Women

I adore Alli, a fiery spirit and mother of five boys. Her authentic spirit bleeds through in *Fierce Faith* as she powerfully translates what it looks like to go to battle with fear, worry, and anxiety and come out victorious. A must read for those ready to take up arms and fight for freedom.

LISA BEVERE, *New York Times* Bestselling Author

So many aspects of our daily lives as women breed perfect opportunities for fear to creep in, anxiety to take hold, or worry to wrestle us to the ground. We dread the future, get all worked up from the pressures of the present, or grow gravely concerned that our past mistakes will haunt us forever. If this describes you, Alli Worthington is about to give you a wonderful gift. *Fierce Faith* is a helpful tool that will empower you to replace the lies of Satan with the truth of God's Word, transforming you from worrier to warrior as you do.

KAREN EHMAN, *New York Times* best-selling author of *Keep It Shut: What to Say, How to Say It and When to Say Nothing at All* and *Listen, Love, Repeat: Other-Centered Living in a Self-Centered World*

Alli uses humor and storytelling to make us all feel as though we're not alone in this battle against fear in our lives. Her step-by-step approach to fighting fear is one that you will find helpful no matter how big or small your worries are!

JAMIE IVEY, podcast host of *The Happy Hour with Jamie Ivey*

Fierce Faith is a timely word to an anxiety-ridden culture. We want to present that we have it all together, yet in truth our fears tear us apart. Alli gets it, and she gets you. In *Fierce Faith*, Alli writes with warmth, compassion, and honesty. But because Alli knows what fear can do, she is not messing around either. She roots us in truth and gives us practical wisdom and tools to live in freedom and courage. When it's time to face the fears that have held you back, you'll need to be fierce. I highly recommend that you take up *Fierce Faith* as one of your companions.

JO SAXTON, speaker, author, podcast cohost of *Lead Stories*, board chair for 3D Movements

You'll read this line in Alli's amazing book: "I needed a battle plan, one that involved spiritual steps as well as physical ones." I knew Alli was an incredible leader and a super-wise gal, but after reading that line I pulled out my pens and highlighters and set my intentions on devouring this book as quickly as possible. I'm so thankful for women like her, giving us the actual tools we need to do battle. This book is one of those incredibly helpful ones that will not disappoint.

JESS CONNOLLY, coauthor of *Wild and Free* and author of *Dance, Stand, Run*

I couldn't help but cheer out loud as I read these practical and powerful pages! *Fierce Faith* will fire you up about living God's truth and free you to flourish right where you are. Move over, fear—a generation of women is about to step out with fierce faith!

LARA CASEY, author of *Make It Happen* and *Cultivate*

Fierce Faith is a humorous, challenging, and yet hopeful guide to wrestling some of our deepest and most personal issues: fear, worry, and anxiety. In typical Alli Worthington style, you'll feel like you're having a personal conversation with a friend who knows you well and is comfortable enough to challenge you to learn, grow, and find God in your most vulnerable moments.

JENNI CATRON, Founder of The 4Sight Group and author
of *The 4 Dimensions of Extraordinary Leadership*

As a woman who's struggled with fear and anxiety most of my life, Alli's words are both a much-needed comfort and a battle cry. She speaks with the voice of an encouraging friend as well as the wisdom and strength of a warrior who wants all of us to be free.

HOLLEY GERTH, author of *Fiercehearted:*
Live Fully, Love Bravely

I love how Alli has created not only a battle plan, but a manual on how to fight fear. Whether real fears or imaginary fears, I feel like I have actionable steps to move forward even if I'm afraid. I've realized that "breaking busy" has allowed me to have "fierce faith"! If you need an action plan for your battle plan, this is your book!

BIANCA JUAREZ OLTHOFF, author, speaker,
and founder of In The Name of Love

The more I speak with Christian women, the more I learn how common feelings of fear, worry, and anxiety are among us. Alli's book *Fierce Faith* has never been more needed by the body of Christ. Offering practical strategies and releasing sound scriptural truth, this isn't a "pray more and you'll feel better" book.

This is a real plan of action to overcome fear for anyone ready to live free.

BECKY THOMPSON, Author of *Hope Unfolding* and *Love Unending*

Fierce Faith is exactly what it claims to be—a trustworthy guide written by a natural teacher. With a voice of poise and compassion, Alli takes you by the hand and guides you into the fear you're facing, teaching you how to debunk it with the power of God on your side. This is a book to keep on the bookshelf for the long haul, returning to the wisdom contained in the pages throughout different seasons of your life.

HANNAH BRENCHER, Founder of More Love Letters, Blogger at HannahBrencher.com, speaker, and author of *If You Find This Letter*

Sometimes it takes one brave soul naming their deepest, darkest fears so that the rest of us can recognize our own. In *Fierce Faith*, Alli does this courageous work, naming our fears and providing practical steps to fight them. Packed with truth, this book will not only help you take down your fears, but it will help you feel normal, understood, and empowered for the fight.

SHARON HODDE MILLER, author of *Free of Me: Why Life Is Better When It's Not about You*

FIERCE
FAITH

FIERCE FAITH

A WOMAN'S GUIDE TO FIGHTING FEAR, WRESTLING WORRY, AND OVERCOMING ANXIETY

ALLI WORTHINGTON

ZONDERVAN

Fierce Faith
Copyright © 2018 by Alli Worthington

Requests for information should be addressed to:
Zondervan, *3900 Sparks Dr. SE, Grand Rapids, Michigan 49546*

ISBN 978-0-310-34993-8 (audio)

ISBN 978-0-310-34226-7 (ebook)

Library of Congress Cataloging-in-Publication Data
Names: Worthington, Alli, author.
Title: Fierce faith : a woman's guide to fighting fear, wrestling worry, and overcoming
    anxiety / Alli Worthington.
Description: Grand Rapids, Michigan : Zondervan, [2018]
Identifiers: LCCN 2017020148 | ISBN 9780310342250 (softcover)
Subjects: LCSH: Christian women — Religious life. | Fear — Religious
    aspects — Christianity.
Classification: LCC BV4527 .W64 2018 | DDC 248.8/43 — dc23 LC record available at
    https://lccn.loc.gov/2017020148

Published in association with literary agent Jenni Burke of D. C. Jacobson & Associates
LLC, an Author Management Company, www.dcjacobson.com.

Art direction: Curt Diepenhorst
Interior design: Denise Froehlich
Editorial team: Sandra Vander Zicht, Lori Vanden Bosch, Gwyneth Findlay

First printing November 2017 / Printed in the United States of America

19 20 21 PC/LSCH 10 9 8 7 6 5

For Mom
Thank you for who you are.
I am so grateful for you.
I love you fiercely.

CONTENTS

CHAPTER 1

FROZEN IN FEAR

I left my house early one morning for a meeting at my boys' school, making sure I had more than enough time to make a Starbucks run and a trip into Target. (Hey, if you have to sit through a volunteer meeting, you might as well have coffee and a pretty notebook, right?)

As I ordered my latte (with an extra shot of espresso, thank you very much) in the drive-thru, "No Longer Slaves" by Bethel Worship started playing. I reached over to the radio and turned up the sound as loud as I could without calling attention to this middle-aged mom bumping worship tunes in a drive-thru.

I love that song so much. Since the first time I heard it, I have to fight the urge to belt it out at the top of my lungs. (My kids wince when they hear me sing, but let's still call it a joyful noise, okay?) As I pulled around the drive-thru, I sang that I was not a slave to fear and that I was a child of God, and without warning the words caught in my throat, this time taking me by surprise on some deeper emotional level than ever before.

"Man, I need that coffee worse than I thought," I said to myself, trying to explain my emotional response to a song I'd sung a thousand times.

I paid for my coffee and headed to Target, but instead of going in, I ended up sitting in the parking lot with that song on repeat. As the song played, I couldn't keep myself from crying.

As I sat and sang about being surrounded by the arms of my

father, I was totally undone by the song. I ugly cried so hard I had to skip the meeting and drive back home.

But I had no idea why I reacted that way.

It wasn't until I talked to my friend Amanda later that day that my eyes were finally opened to what had happened in that Target parking lot. As I told her about the song and why I was a no-show at the meeting, I said, "It struck a chord in me like never before. I mean, I just about tear up *every time* I sing that song, but today was different, and I have no idea why."

"Alli," she said, "I think I understand why that song wrecked you. You are completely bound up by fear and worry right now. I see how it weighs you down, and honestly, I don't know how you live like that. It's as if you try to make safety your god. You have to decide if you are going to learn to live out from under the rock of fear you carry around."

I was, of course, appalled and slightly offended. I'm a grown woman. I'm thirty-nine years old, have five children and a happy marriage, and I even wrote a book about living life well. I think I would know if I were completely weighed down by fear and worry. (And if you are wondering if I was feeling a little too big for my britches right then—the answer is yes, yes, I was.)

When we try to make safety our god, we live life stuck in fear and worship a powerless god.

But Amanda is a good friend (yes, we're still friends), and someone I turn to for real talk and wise counsel. She is full of wisdom and understanding, and she's a woman who knows and loves Jesus. When she speaks, I listen. And as much as I hated to say it, she was exactly right.

With my eyes open to this truth, I had to wonder when had I become so overwhelmed by fear and worry, so overwhelmed, in fact, that I had become blind to it? Were there warning signs along the way I had missed?

My response to the song was my soul declaring it wanted to be free, no longer a slave to fear.

Breaking Busy and Breaking Down

Now here's the deal: I have faced some seriously hard things in my life, including losing my dad in a horrible car accident when I was a young child, and my husband and I losing everything we owned in bankruptcy with five young boys at home. You'd think I'd be fearless because of the hardships I've faced. I've seen God provide manna in the midst of famine after famine in my life.

I know he provides. I've seen him do it over and over again, but despite all that, I was full of fear. People have often told me I *am* fearless and brave and confident, but that's the armor I've always put on to convince myself that I am. The reality is that for most of my life, I avoided what made me feel uncomfortable and ran away from what made me worry. I lived my life frozen in fear, weighed down by worry and absorbed in my anxiety.

I guess I thought my fear and worry were normal. I assumed we all lived under the weight of worry. That it was just a consequence of living in the world. Most of the time I was able to manage it. I could hide it well enough to convince myself and others I had it all together, but inside fear and worry were eating away at me.

When *Breaking Busy* launched on January 26, 2016, from the outside looking in, I seemed to be in a pretty sweet spot. I had a great family and a wonderful job. As a first-time author, this small-town girl had made it big. I was sitting on top of the world.

But things were a lot harder and a lot scarier in real life than they appeared on the outside.

My husband, Mark, three years earlier developed a severe form of adult onset asthma, a disease that rocked our world. It took a terrifying year and a half for us to even get the correct diagnosis and the right medicines that allowed him to breathe clearly every day.

We had settled in with the new normal of dealing with the chronic illness, until that January, when his illness took a drastic turn for the worse. Every cold virus the boys brought home wreaked havoc on his health. A small cold for one of our boys would turn into a two- or three-week serious illness for Mark, an illness that required a machine to help him breathe and a series of new medicines.

In early January, he was given a new medicine that caused terrible side effects. It was truly a case of the cure being worse than the disease. Unfortunately, we didn't realize that the new medicine was making Mark so sick, so as he took more of the medication, he got sicker and sicker with side effects that affected every area of his health.

By the time *Breaking Busy* came out, we were both beaten down by the illness and its effects. Every aspect of our lives, including our marriage, was a struggle due to the health challenges. We were in a place where we worried things might never get better.

As more and more difficulties piled on, I found myself saying things like "I can't handle this. I don't want to do this anymore." Or "Why us? Why now?" The seeds of fear and hopelessness had been planted in our hearts during Mark's extended illness, and they were growing into thick weeds of despair.

As I worked to keep my head above water caring for my family, and with my work, I lived in fear that people would think I was a fraud. My life was in shambles. *Breaking Busy* promised women they could find peace in a world of crazy busy, but my life was anything but peaceful.

As things became harder and harder for us, I told myself that I couldn't handle it, that things were only going to get worse, that we were helpless as the storm spun around us. My hopelessness began to make me sink in the middle of that storm.

The week the book released to the world, my friend Christine Caine called me early one morning to encourage me and give me a message.

"Girlfriend, I need to talk to you. With *Breaking Busy*, you are taking territory from the enemy. You are on the front lines of this battle. The devil is going to come against you in any way he can. He's going to attack your boys. He's going to attack Mark. You must be strong, and you have to fight."

I started crying. You see, I'm not really a fighter. I'm a flee-er. It's not my nature to turn and face a storm head on. I talk a big game, but truth be told, at the first sign of a strong wind, I'm running for the closet. I want to hide in a corner and wait until the storm passes. Didn't she know I've lived my life hiding under the covers as the storms roll by?

And here she was telling me to be strong and to fight? I didn't even know what fighting would look like!

> We are all called to be strong and courageous.

I interrupted Christine, choking back my tears and telling her that Mark was sicker than he had been in years, that everything was falling apart, and that I was so scared of what the future would bring.

Christine didn't miss a beat. She continued, "Listen to me. Do not back down. You are in a battle. I'm telling you to fight. Don't hide in the corner and eat Reese's Peanut Butter Cups. This is the time to be strong and courageous. Do not back down."

The more I thought about her words, and the words of my friend Amanda, I realized I had been cowering in the corner, living a life of worry, overcome by my fear. These messages from dear friends were my call to arms.

It was time for this scared girl to learn how to fight.

The Body and the Spirit

As Christians, we have the absolutely amazing experience of living life in our physical bodies while being filled with the Holy Spirit. We literally live on two levels.

We are beings made out of both body and spirit, the physical and the spiritual. My spirit knows that the victory is in Jesus. My spirit knows that I have nothing to fear. My spirit knows that the God of heaven and earth loves me and wants the best for me. My spirit is empowered by the Holy Spirit who is our comforter and strength.

But my body lives in the physical world, and my body is flat out scared. My body tells me to run and hide. My body tells me to avoid sticky situations. My body tells me to believe only what I can see.

There is a battle between the spiritual and the physical. When the spirit says, "Perfect love casts out fear," my body replies, "But I'm still scared."

For a long time this battle between the spiritual and the physical made me question myself.

Did I not have enough faith?

Did I not love Jesus enough?

What was wrong with me?

Why, when the Bible was so clear that I was to be anxious for nothing, did I still worry?

I have heard a hundred sermons encouraging me to trust more and fear less. But I still woke up in the middle of the night worried about my kids.

I've read books telling me that to be fearless I just needed to have more faith, and yet, on hard days, I walked around with knots of anxiety in my stomach, thinking about all the *what-if*s.

Spiritually, I needed to learn to trust God more and rest in the knowledge that he loves me and will take care of me. Physically,

I needed practical weapons to help me fight the daily battles. I needed a battle plan, one that involved spiritual steps as well as physical ones.

Armed with the realization that I was living a life of fear and encouraged to fight for freedom, I made discoveries about myself and about the fear, worries, and anxiety that torment me, and probably you too.

Paul teaches us, "For the flesh desires what is contrary to the Spirit, and the Spirit what is contrary to the flesh. They are in conflict with each other" (Galatians 5:17). In other words, we have a fight on our hands.

Just as we exist on two levels, I had to learn to fight on two levels, both the spiritual and the physical. I'm going to share with you exactly what I learned: the truth I found in Scripture, the peace I found in Jesus, and the practical steps I learned to wrestle worry to the ground and show fear who was in charge.

How Fear, Anxiety, and Worry Affect Us

Here are a few things I'm learning about fear.

1. Fear turns your *what-ifs* into certainties

Fear is a liar. It speaks over us so convincingly, we believe that something terrible is certain to happen, even in the absence of any evidence whatsoever. Fear turns our *what-ifs* into certainties, freezing our faith and flipping our world upside down.

Fear is the most effective tool the enemy has in this world, and Jesus knew that would be the case. That's why he tells us 121 times in the Gospels alone to "fear not." And that's why he taught about fear on twenty-one different occasions. He knew this would be our struggle!

Does your world ever feel flipped upside down?

2. Fear causes you to doubt God

John 10:10 says, "The thief comes to steal, kill, and destroy." But what does he come to steal, kill, and destroy? He comes to steal, kill, and destroy our love of God, our peace, our happiness, and our trust in his love and goodness. The enemy's objective is literally to replace God on his throne. When he causes us to fear, we doubt God and believe fear. When we believe fear, we are believing the enemy, who, according to John 8:44, is the author of lies.

Do you ever doubt God?

3. Fear keeps you focused on yourself

We are meant to grow, to become the people we are created to be, to continually be moving forward in our faith. We are a work in progress. None of us is perfect. Fear tells us we must live a certain way or we will be judged, rejected, and possibly even abandoned altogether. So our focus is continually on ourselves. And for most of us, fear causes us to beat ourselves up over every little thing. When we believe fear, it keeps us from living authentic lives, lives meant to be a testimony of God's grace and goodness.

Do you worry what people would think if they
knew the details of your "real" life?

4. Fear keeps you from enjoying life

It is so easy to hold tightly onto the things that are dear to us: our homes, our jobs, our marriages, our kids. Surrender is not an easy thing, to be sure. When we trust God, and trust his love and mercy for us, surrender is easier, but our human nature is to want what we want. Fear tells us to hold on *for dear life* to the things that are dear to us. Believing this keeps us from enjoying life because we are so busy trying to control everything.

*Do you feel the need to control things in your life,
especially your family and your children?*

If you answered yes to any of these questions, then I want you to know you are in good company. It means you are human. We all share the need to feel loved, accepted, and safe.

Even though we don't often talk about it with our friends or even like to think about it, most of us do struggle with fear, anxiety, and worry.

We are so blind to our fear, we don't even like to use the word *fear*. We say, "I'm worried about..." or "I'm stressed over ..." when actually we are feeling afraid. Fear is so scary that we don't even like to say the word!

> We all share the need to be loved, to belong, and to stop feeling so afraid all the time.

Here's the low-down, friends: to be human is to feel fear. But we don't have to let fear overwhelm us.

It's Time to Fight

I learned fear and worry weren't the things stopping me in my daily life. The problem was me living life to avoid them. Until I learned to fight back against the storms of worry, I would be a slave to fear. A slave of my own making.

But friend, it's time to fight, time to break free of fear, to cast off our anxieties and win the war against worry. It's time for *you* to fight, time to battle the things that scare you, things that keep you up at night with worry, the anxieties that steal today's joy by getting you to focus on tomorrow's problems.

I believe wholeheartedly that these words are in your hands because you too are called to this battle. This entire book is a battle plan against the fear, worry, and anxiety that weigh you down. In each chapter, you will find strategies for fighting specific fears and in the final section you will find step-by-step exercises that you can use to build your faith and your confidence.

Fierce Faith is our call to arms. As women of God, our battle is not against the things of this world, but powers and forces in the spiritual realm.

Instead of letting fear and worry overwhelm us, let's use the battle plan in your hands to fight back. Instead of living our lives under the weight of worry, let's learn the way to overcome. Let's trade hiding from what scares us for really believing the promises of God deep inside us. Let's trade in our defense mechanisms and learn to live bravely.

Your fears and worries may look different than mine. You may worry that you will fail or that someone will betray or reject you or that the money will run out or that something bad will happen to your children. We all carry the weight of fear.

Everyone's burden is unique, but I promise you, we are all carrying our own weight. The good news is we don't have to suffer under this weight alone. We are created to live free from the fear, anxiety, and worries that the enemy tries to burden us with.

Fear freezes our faith. But when we fight, our faith frees us from fear.

The enemy is not going to stop fighting and neither will we. We can fight confidently because we know the enemy is defeated, the war has already been won, and it's our job to fight the battles with strength and confidence. Fear may freeze our faith. But when we fight, and oh, we *will* fight, our faith frees us from fear.

You don't have to live life frozen in fear. Together, we can stand on the truth of who God says we are. Powerful and armed by him, and with him, for battle.

I want us all to be able to sing with confidence that we have walked right through the middle of the sea, our fears replaced with fierce faith.

Action Steps

Ask yourself the four questions in italics in the "How Fear, Anxiety, and Worry Affects Us" section above. Do any of these questions resonate?

- What type of fears and worries affect you most often?
- How have you dealt with fear and worry in the past? Is your natural inclination to fight, to flee, or to hide?
- What is one thing you can do today to change how you respond to fear?

CHAPTER 2

THE FIVE BAD B'S

The Not-So-Healthy Ways
We Respond to Fear

When you have a giant family, like I do, you do things differently than the average family. Because we have five sons, our cars are bigger, the grocery carts are always spilling over, and the laundry never gets caught up (or put away completely, but that's a story for another day). Likewise, our vacations look different than the average family's. With seven of us, we really can't just jet off on a plane and take a big family vacation. The plane tickets alone would eat up most of our vacation budget.

One year, though, my mother-in-law gave us the vacation of a lifetime to Disney World. I love all things Disney, and amusement parks are my favorite thing, so it was a double win. (Clearly I was only thinking about the kids here!) I wanted everything to be absolutely perfect. We were going to do it all, see it all, and make the best magical memories ever.

We all know what it's like if you're a mother trying to get a family ready to go on vacation. Not only did I have to pack my stuff, pack the kids' stuff, do all the laundry, eat all the food in the fridge, arrange for pet care, and clean the house, I also had to wrap up my work responsibilities for the week I would be gone. Being out of touch for a week gave me anxiety just thinking about it!

The night before our trip, Mark (the proverbial early bird, bless him) announced we needed to leave for our ten-hour drive at 5:00 a.m. I was already rushing around the house, feeling the pressure to get it all done, so I made a big mug of hot tea for just a little dose of caffeine to keep going.

Meanwhile, in the living room, the younger boys were playing a game they call "Ziplining Lovies," where they tie a spool of thread from the wrought-iron spindles of our second-story catwalk to the doorknobs of the family room below. Then they race the lovies (small stuffed animals) down the ziplines. As far as kid games go, this one's a winner; there is no wrestling, jumping off furniture, or potential broken bones involved. It was the perfect way for them to play while I ran around the house getting everything ready.

You sense where this is heading, don't you?

I set my cup of tea on the coffee table and sat down to fold clothes fresh from the dryer. Of course, just then, "Big Beaver" came barreling down from above, knocking my tea straight into the basket of clean laundry that I'd been planning to pack.

Ughhhh!

The boys roared with hoots, hollers, and laughter (because they are boys and a beaver crashing into things is kind of funny), but I'm pretty sure flames shot right out of these crazy curls of mine. "*What are you guys doing?* Can't you see I'm trying to get us ready to go on vacation? We are going to the *happiest place on earth*. Can't you at least be grateful and not make it harder for me to get everything done? Do you even want to go on vacation? We can stay home. *Do you want to just not go?* Well, let me tell you what, boys, if we can't leave in the morning, you will know why. *Because I can't get us ready now!* That's why!"

The boys went silent. Mark peeked his head out of the kitchen, not saying a word, and the teenage boys opened their bedroom doors to see what in the world had happened. I don't lose my cool very often, and normally I would have laughed about the tea and made the boys clean it up themselves. I looked at them all staring at me post flip-out, spun around to stomp off, and burst into tears. I was mad at my sons, and I was mad at myself. I threw myself down on my bed and immediately regretted getting angry and yelling at them. After all, they were playing a game they have played a hundred times, and I was the one who left my tea on the coffee table. My flip-out was completely over the top!

I realize now that the root of my freaking out over the "great beaver tea incident," as we now call it, was frustration and fear. I was afraid that something would go wrong while we were away: the house would burn down, the neighbor would forget to take care of our dog Mollie, an emergency would pop up at work that I would have to address, and on and on and on. I was worried I wouldn't get everything done and worried that even if I did, something would still go wrong. The fear-filled worries were playing in a loop in my head.

That's the thing about fear. Fear doesn't have to stem from some catastrophic event that cripples us. Fear often stems from small worries and anxiety that build up over time, eventually shutting us down or causing us to explode.

> Everyday worries can be as crippling as catastrophes.

Psychologists have wrestled with definitions of fear, anxiety, and worry. They have broken them down in great detail, finding the various differences for each. I'll leave that to the professionals. For me, and for many of the hundreds of women I've talked to, fear, anxiety, and worry are just all rolled up into a big messy ball of heartache. So when I use the word *fear,* know that it covers worry and anxiety as well.

The Five Bad B's

Isn't it interesting that before Amanda pointed out that I was bound by fear, I didn't realize how affected I was? I had myself convinced I was managing it well. I have written blog posts about being fearless. I've written forewords to books and given interviews about being fearless. I have even jokingly said, "I'm Internet Alli, and Internet Alli is fearless!" (We can all feel brave and fearless when we are behind our iPhone and laptop screens, right?) Turns out, I am an expert in fear. If there were a PhD program in fear, you would be calling me "Dr. Worthington." I just assumed the anxiety and worry that so often had me frozen were just normal life, something everyone went through. I literally had no idea I *needed* or *could* be free of the worry that followed me around like a dark cloud. I didn't realize that fear was keeping me from what God had for me in my life. But isn't that the way the enemy works? He blinds us to the things we need to see in our lives and rejoices when we are blissfully unaware.

That's why the first step to fighting fear is naming it—just recognizing it in ourselves! We have an amazing ability to avoid naming our fear and calling it out for what it is. Instead, when we feel afraid, we tend to respond in unhealthy ways. These unhealthy coping strategies for dealing with our fear help us numb our negative feelings until we reach the point where we are unaware that we have these feelings at all!

I like to call these unconscious coping strategies for fear "The Five Bad B's." Let's take a closer look at each one.

1. Busy

When we feel anxious, a common coping strategy is to stay busy to distract ourselves from our worries. For almost a year, when I needed to have a conversation with a friend to address something uncomfortable, the fear of her disappointment or anger felt overwhelming. Instead of actually talking to her, I filled my days with meetings whenever we were in the same office so I would magically be "too busy" to make the time to talk to her.

Making ourselves busy is one of the most common and most dangerous coping mechanisms we use to avoid the things in our lives that stress us out.

Do any of these sound familiar?

- Your marriage is a struggle, so you immerse yourself in the busyness of raising children to avoid the problems.
- You are "volunteer of the year of good causes" as a way to cover the guilt of neglecting other responsibilities that stress you out.
- You over-focus on small, accomplishable tasks rather than facing and tackling the looming big stuff. (Why address those worries at work when there are kids' socks that need to be matched?)

In *Breaking Busy*, I wrote, "The more we worry, give in to fear, or think negatively about ourselves, the busier we get. We are driven to do more, be more, in order to prevent whatever it is we are worried about."[1]

As the adage goes, "If the devil can't make you bad, he'll make you busy."

The root of your busyness might be the seed of fear you've sown in your heart.

When you find yourself getting busier and busier, stop and ask yourself, what is driving this busyness? You'll likely find the root of it is fear.

2. Blame

A few weeks ago, one of my sons was worried about taking a spelling test. He gets a fair amount of test anxiety, even when he knows the material. That morning I tried to do something special, so I made pancakes for breakfast. (I'm a master at weekday cereal pouring or oatmeal making. This was real cooking before 7:00 a.m.—a big deal.) When I greeted him with the surprise breakfast, he tearfully said, "I don't like pancakes for breakfast! They make me sleepy. Now I'm going to do terrible on the test!"

Clearly my kind gesture of making pancakes did not ruin his morning, nor would eating them cause him to fail his spelling test. He was trying to ease his own momentary fear and anxiety by blaming me for something unrelated.

Blaming others when we feel anxious or worried is a common coping mechanism. It is as if our brains are saying, "I can't handle feeling this way, and I need to take it out on someone else," so we shift our focus to others instead of focusing on the problem at hand.

This is exactly what I did to my boys in the "great beaver tea incident." I tried to blame them for the fact that I was afraid I couldn't get us ready in time to go.

If you too find yourself blaming others, you might be using blame to overcome your worry.

3. Binge

Bingeing is the act of doing something to excess. It can take the form of excessive eating (Hello, Reese's Peanut Butter Cups!), exercising, drinking, shopping, or any number of other acts of bingeing. And bingeing is a very common way of coping with our feelings of fear and stress.

A new form of unhealthy bingeing is binge-watching TV. The danger here is that you are not only overindulging in something to avoid your anxiety, but you are also ignoring your life around you. Research shows that bingeing on TV for hours and hours a day may make us feel more stressed, anxious, and depressed.[2]

If we have habits that are directly related to stressful situations in our lives, and they are not renewing or restoring us, then we need to recognize those choices as warning signs of unaddressed fear.

4. Bury

We bury our feelings in three primary ways: through denial, procrastination, and avoidance—and often these three ways become intertwined with one another.

- Denial

    Pretending that something just doesn't exist is a form of burying our fear. If it's not real, or we can convince ourselves it isn't real, then we don't have to deal with it. I had a good friend whose mom died from breast cancer. One day, shortly after her annual physical, my friend was doing a self-exam and discovered a tiny lump in her breast. She told herself, "You are just worried you're going to get breast cancer too, so now you are imagining things." Still in denial, she put off going to the doctor or asking for a mammogram. As you might guess, she did have a cancerous lump, and her breast cancer was fairly advanced by the time a doctor discovered it.

- Procrastination

    Procrastinators are excellent buriers. I know because I was the queen of procrastinating and making myself busy to avoid problems. If you admit you have a fear, but put off dealing with it, you are probably burying some worry that needs to be faced.

- Avoidance

    Sometimes, when fear or anxiety looms so large, we just try to avoid it altogether. This happened to me years ago in my business. We were going through some lean months, and the bills were piling up. I began to avoid checking the bank account. My anxiety about how much money was going into the account versus how much was leaving the account was so overwhelming that I just wanted to avoid it altogether. I can tell you from experience, ignoring your bank account balance doesn't magically make it have more money, but it *can* cause you to overdraw your account.

Burying our fears allows us to focus on little, unimportant things. It allows us to feel in control instead of dealing with the situations that scare or upset us the most.

5. Brood

Brooding is replaying in our minds what has happened or what could happen, over and over again. The experts call this rumination, and it causes depression and anxiety.

Rumination means thinking about a specific issue at great length; in other words, overthinking it or obsessing about it. A cow ruminates when it chews its cud. A mouthful of food at a time comes back up from the cow's stomach into its mouth and the cow chews it over

Brooding is like watching a bad movie stuck on repeat.

and over and over. That's gross, but think about it in terms of worrying about past or future events. Essentially, when you brood, your brain keeps "throwing up" your anxiety, and you keep feasting on it over and over and over again.

When we get stuck brooding over bad things that happened in the past or potential bad things that could happen in the future, we can't move on and do what we need to do in life. The more we brood over something, the worse we feel. We get stuck in an anxiety loop and end up feeling frozen in fear.

In my early years in business, I used to often struggle with brooding over any mistakes I made. I would forget to send an email to follow up on a phone meeting I had with someone. This person would have to email me about it first, which in the grand scheme of things wasn't really a big deal, but it would trigger a downward spiral of unhealthy thinking.

I shouldn't have forgotten; people are depending on me to manage everything. I can't make a mistake. If I don't do a good job others won't be able to depend on me. I'm not doing a good job, I can't do this. I'm in over my head. I shouldn't let things slip through the cracks. And my thoughts would go on and on in a downward spiral of negativity. This, my friend, was brooding at its finest!

Bad B's in the Bible

It is common to avoid battling our fear and instead busy ourselves, blame others, binge away our concerns, bury our worries, or brood until we are an emotional mess. Since the beginning of time we have been coping with fear by using the Five Bad B's. (I mean literally from the beginning of time.) Here are a few friends from the Bible who show us we are not alone in our struggles to cope with fear.

The Busy Body

Martha, the people pleaser, was the queen of busy. She lived in fear of letting people down and losing control. Remember when Jesus came to visit, and she worked feverishly on all the details of the meal? That chicken wasn't going to fry itself, you know. Eventually, she got mad at her sister, Mary, for slacking, and even tried to have Jesus tell her sister to get to work. If we aren't careful, fear can keep us so busy that we will miss out on the incredible moments God has in store for us.

The Blamer

Hands down one of my favorite blame moments in the Bible is when Adam and Eve ate the forbidden fruit from the tree of knowledge and went and hid from God out of fear. I don't know what Adam feared, maybe it was fear of someone seeing his naked body (can I get an amen? I'm scared of that too!) or maybe it was just the fear that God would be disappointed in him. But the first thing Adam said when confronted by God was, "It's that woman you gave me, Lord." What I think is so funny is that Adam is hiding in fear of God, but the first person he blames for his predicament *is* God!

The Binger

The prodigal son suffered from a severe case of FOMO, the fear of missing out, so much so that he asked his dad for his inheritance so he could go binge on all that life had to offer. I can picture the prodigal son living it up, raising his fist in the air and shouting, "You only live once!" But I can also picture that moment when he realized his fear of missing out (and his bingeing because of it) caused him to miss out on something even more important: the loving presence of his own father.

The Buriers

There are so many examples of characters in the Bible who denied, procrastinated, and avoided, all so they could bury their fear.

- There's Peter, who was so afraid of being arrested and killed that he actually *denied* he even knew Jesus not once, not twice, but three times!
- Then of course there was Pharaoh, the ultimate *procrastinator*. He *knew* he should let the Israelites go, but he was so afraid of losing power (and free labor) that he kept putting off the inevitable—with catastrophic results.

- And then there was Jonah, the *avoider*. Nahum 3:1–4 makes it pretty clear how wicked the people of Nineveh were. Those guys were huge jerks. Jonah had every reason to be afraid they would attack and kill him if he delivered God's message to them, so he tried to avoid the situation altogether and hopped on a boat to Tarshish (and we all know how *that* worked out).

The Brooder

When the people in town started singing that King Saul had killed thousands of men, but David had killed tens of thousands, Saul became obsessed with his fear of losing power and control, and David became the object of his hate. Eventually, however, Saul's brooding and lack of trust in God led to his ultimate downfall.

A Better Way

Martha was up to her elbows in dishwater and disappointment, Adam got kicked out of the garden, Jonah got swallowed by a whale, and Saul lost his mind, all because of fear. And when each of them was confronted by their fear and the toll it had taken on their lives, the moment of truth was devastating. Had any of them gone to God first, I imagine their stories would have turned out very differently.

Thank God he doesn't want us stuck in our own patterns of denial and avoidance. In fact, he often uses our fearful moments to shake us up and make us turn to him. So then, just like all those great characters in the Bible, we have a choice. Will we continue to busy ourselves, blame others, binge, bury, and brood, all in an effort to squelch our fear and pretend we have everything under control? Or will we turn to him, name our fears, and allow him to teach us a better way to cope?

Action Steps

Check out page 207 for a list of the Five Bad B's. You'll also find a link to print your own copy of the Five Bad B's to keep you on track. (I have a copy on the fridge at home to help the whole family recognize them and fight them!)

- Which of the Five Bad B's do you use most often to numb your fear: busy, blame, bury, binge, or brood?
- Can you think of a time when God opened your eyes to a fear you had and forced you to face it? What happened?

CHAPTER 3

FIGHTING FEAR

Preparing a Battle Plan

Living with any type of ongoing illness can be a struggle for those afflicted and for the family around them. In our case, with Mark's severe adult-onset asthma, the cause for his illness was a mystery and the treatment plan ever-changing, both of which left us feeling out of control.

One week Mark would be perfectly healthy, with the maintenance medicines working great, and life was normal. But if any virus made it into our house (hello, five boys), life essentially stopped and our only focus was on keeping Mark's lungs clear. Every illness settled into his chest, filling his lungs and causing continual bouts of bronchitis and pneumonia. A high fever would set in, and ultimately we were all seized with an overwhelming fear that he wouldn't be able to get enough oxygen into his body.

As I've said, we were in the middle of an "illness episode" when *Breaking Busy* came out, and I had to cancel interviews and appearances until my mom flew in to Nashville to help care for the boys. There I was, telling everyone how to find peace and purpose, but my heart was heavy with worry for my family. I stayed up at night worried about Mark and worried about when the next episode would strike.

What if I were away when he was sick and he didn't take

the right medicines on time? What if his oxygen levels were too low and no one was there to notice and get him help? What if he needed to go to the emergency room but thought he could handle it at home? How would the boys feel seeing Dad so sick without me there to help them understand it all and tell them everything was going to be okay?

Each time I booked a work trip or speaking engagement, I panicked, worried Mark would be sick and I would have to cancel. What if I kept canceling and let everyone down? What if it put my career at risk? How would we pay for the medicines and hospital visits? It was overwhelming. So overwhelming, in fact, that I stopped making plans of any kind and lived in perpetual survival mode.

I called Amanda and told her I was afraid to schedule anything because I wasn't sure what the future even held anymore. She said, "Alli, that is fear talking again."

I said, "No, it isn't, that is me being responsible. I'm the breadwinner, caretaker, and mom! It's my job to see potential situations in the future and plan for them. I'm not scared, I'm responsible!"

Amanda took a breath and said **Don't let the fear of tomorrow steal your life today.** in her matter-of-fact tone, "You can't put your life on hold just in case Mark gets sick. You still have to do your work. You can't let the paralyzing fear of *what-if* keep you frozen. You are letting the fear of tomorrow steal your life today."

And in that moment, I remembered what Christine said when she called and encouraged me: "You have to fight. Don't hide from this."

The fear of *what-if* was stealing my joy even when Mark wasn't sick. I spent every day worried and anxious about when the next episode might happen instead of being thankful for his present health and remission.

One spring day, I walked to my car from the pharmacy after picking up a whole slew of medicines for a severe asthmatic episode and the pneumonia it had caused. As I walked to my car, big tears rolled silently down my cheeks.

Crying for Mark as he suffered another bout of illness.

Crying for the boys, who all became sad, grumpy, and tense when Dad was sick.

Crying for myself because of how hard the next two weeks of illness were going to be.

Crying because I didn't want life to be like this anymore.

I sat in my car, once again crying, overwhelmed with fear.

How am I going to take care of everything?

How am I ever going to pay all the medical bills?

How am I going to keep working and take care of everyone?

With my forehead resting on the steering wheel I prayed desperately:

Lord, this is the worst. Please help me walk through this with grace.

Help me do everything you've called me to do.

Help me be strong and courageous.

Help me see that you work out all things for good.

Help me not focus only on myself.

Help me be brave for the family.

Help me not get stuck in unhealthy thoughts and behaviors.

Help me fight this fear that is on me so I find your peace through this storm.

Help me. Please, I am begging you to help me.

And then I decided to attack this fear by actually doing something. Instead of wiping my tears away, telling myself to buck up, and driving home with a stiff upper lip like I normally would do, I decided to fight back with worship.

I was going to worship even though everything in me felt like my world was crashing in.

I sat right there in that pharmacy parking lot, radio on, singing worship songs through my tears. I sang over my life that I was no longer a slave to fear, that God was a good, good Father, that he was my anchor in the storm, that I was not alone, and that he was the God of miracles and that I believed in him with everything in me.

I sang those songs until I finally started feeling whole again. I sang until my fear and anger turned to reluctant peace. I sang from my spirit until my body believed it.

It would've been awesome if in that moment I heard from Jesus, if he appeared in my passenger seat and chatted with me, or if when I got home I found Mark miraculously healed. None of those things happened, but over the next few months God gave me the strength I prayed for that day.

Sometimes the illness or disability isn't cured, the financial hardships aren't resolved, the bad news doesn't change, but when we throw ourselves at Jesus's feet, he gives us what we need to walk through our difficult seasons and to fight against the storms that darken our skies.

What the Bible Says

Healthy fear can keep us out of painful situations, like shark attacks or Brazilian bikini waxes. But we aren't talking about God-given, healthy fear here. We're talking about fear of the future, the *what-if* situations that keep us up at night worrying, the anxiety that keeps us from living a life with confidence. We are talking about the God-*distracting* fear that steals our joy and keeps us off the path we are meant to follow.

God created our body to sense when it is in danger and to respond physically to that fear. At the first sign of danger, our whole body wakes up to try to keep us safe: our senses sharpen, our hearts beat faster, and blood flow actually increases so we can run away quickly.

Keep in mind, God designed that system for *our good*. But what happens when we become bound by what could only be described as a spirit of fear, a sense that impending doom is *always* around the corner?

God-given, healthy fear protects us from harm.

Second Timothy 1:7 says, "For God has not given us a spirit of fear, but of power and of love and of a sound mind."

God-distracting, unhealthy fear steals our joy.

Does living a life where you filter everything in survival mode sound like a spirit of power and love and a sound mind? Of course not. A spirit of fear is something the enemy uses to twist what God created for our good, because that's what the enemy does. And I know it's not always fun or cool to talk about the enemy, but all we have to do is look at Scripture and know he is there. "For our struggle is not against flesh and blood, but against the rulers, against the authorities, against the powers of this dark world and against the spiritual forces of evil in the heavenly realms" (Ephesians 6:12).

I don't believe we need to live our lives preoccupied with our enemy, but we need to be wise and know how to fight his attacks. Pretending he doesn't exist is foolishness. And ignoring that he is constantly looking for ways to destroy our trust in God, our lives, and our joy is like living life with no coffee: My eyes might be open, but I'm not very alert, and I'm definitely not bringing my A game.

The enemy creates a spirit of fear in us by infiltrating our thoughts and convincing us of things that flat-out aren't true. It's why we have to pay attention to our mindset on an ongoing basis. Whether you are nineteen or ninety, the quality of your thoughts will directly affect the quality of your life.

Healthy thoughts will give us a life that has hope and happiness.

Unhealthy thoughts will give us a life bound by worry and sadness.

Think about it: each of the five ways we try to deal with fear (the Bad B's) are all thought patterns. Our thoughts create our realities.

It's why learning the tools to fight fear is so important. In fact, I believe it is our responsibility to fight. When we don't fight, we let the enemy win. But the great news is, we are powerful in this fight because "the weapons we fight with are not the weapons of the world. On the contrary, they have divine power to demolish strongholds. We demolish arguments and every pretension that sets itself up against the knowledge of God, and we take captive every thought to make it obedient to Christ" (2 Corinthians 10:4–5).

Our thoughts have the power to tear us down or build us up.

A Battle Plan to Fight Fear

When the fear, worry, and anxiety comes, and you know it will, we have to be ready for the fight. Simply saying "I'm going to fight fear" isn't going to be enough to win. We need a plan of attack. (I don't know why, but when I wrote that, I pictured a pirate saying, "Arrgh. We need a plan!")

These are the four main weapons I use to battle fear and walk through difficult situations and tough seasons. I believe God taught me these after my breakdown in the pharmacy parking lot that day.

They are small steps, but the biggest improvements come with the smallest changes.

Often we believe the lie that to turn a painful situation around we have to work even harder, develop a long to-do list, and change everything about life. This sounds about as fun as a colonoscopy. But give these four small steps a try, and I promise you that your life will never be the same.

When you feel wrecked by worry or frozen in fear, battle the Five Bad B's with the Four Good A's. (It's cheesy, but it works!)

1. Aware (Be aware of your feelings)

That day in the pharmacy parking lot, I was so wrecked with worry I wasn't even aware I was crying until the tears dripped onto my hands. If I had continued to stuff my feelings, roll up my sleeves, and take care of everyone and everything like a robot, I would not have cried out to God that I needed his help. Once I was aware of my feelings, my breakdown led to a breakthrough.

Because of the severity of Mark's illness, I secretly felt guilty and selfish at my own level of frustration, fear, and sadness. "I'm not the one who is sick, after all," I thought. I was playing the dangerous game of judging **Breakdowns bring** whose pain and suffering mattered more. **breakthroughs.** Sometimes we make the mistake of thinking our feelings aren't as important or valid as other people's, but that is absolutely not true.

Our feelings come from a combination of what we think and what we believe. I felt sad and overwhelmed due to constant negative thoughts about this season of our lives, and my belief deep down inside that things were never going to get better.

I had to admit what I was feeling so I could start to heal.

Feelings are the way we know the health of our thoughts. When we are aware of our feelings, it helps them not be able sneak up on us and sideswipe us.

Have you ever found yourself overwhelmed all of a sudden and wondering how your emotions bowled you over? Sometimes it is because we have been bottling up our emotions for so long.

Being aware allows us to be self-compassionate instead of self-critical. Giving ourselves permission to feel, and acknowledging our true feelings, is the first step to battling our fear.

2. Avoid the Five B's (Don't numb your feelings)

My go-to coping behavior every time Mark had an especially difficult episode was some combination of the bad B's. I stayed busy with his medical care, housework, my own work, and taking care of the kids. I rushed from one thing to another from the time my feet hit the floor in the morning to when my head hit the pillow at night. I told myself my constant activity was necessary, but the truth is, I stayed busy because when I sat down, the fear, sadness, and anxiety would overwhelm me.

When I wasn't busy, I was brooding. I focused on every *what-if* scenario that could possibly happen. What if Mark never got better? What if the boys were traumatized from seeing Dad sick for so long? *What if, what if, what if* was on a constant loop in my mind.

On the days I couldn't handle it anymore, I buried my fears in a bag of Reese's Peanut Butter Cups and binge-watched movies late at night. I convinced myself I needed an outlet, and that was my go-to coping outlet of choice. But slowly I've learned to be aware of when I am using the Bad B's and to avoid them. When I feel myself getting busy, or burying, or binging, or any of the other B's, I stop, pray, and then ask myself, "Are my fears causing me to behave this way?"

Being aware of your fear, and aware of your tendencies to cope with the Five Bad B's, can help you avoid them.

3. Ask Jesus for help (Take it to Jesus and let him fight the spiritual battle)

We need to ask for a clear mind, peaceful heart, and extra strength and courage on our most trying days. Our most powerful tools will always be prayer and worship. We know spiritually that we should take everything to Jesus, that the battle is his and that we fight not *for* a victory, but from the place of an *already won* victory.

With my forehead on the steering wheel, crying out to Jesus for help, I was saying, "I can't do this alone, I've been pretending like I am alone in this, and I need you." I begged for the ability to have faith and believe wholeheartedly that he was in control and would work out all things for my good.

How do you ask Jesus for help? It's different for everyone. I often use simple prayer—just talking to Jesus from the heart. I also sing worship songs to him, and speak aloud certain Psalms (Psalm 1, 34, 37, and 139 are some of my favorites).

You might go to Jesus by journaling your prayers, or you may also seek the support of Christian friends or a wise counselor, or read the Bible and inspirational devotionals or books (like this one!). There have been so many times in my life that Jesus has spoken to me through my good friends, given me just what I needed for the day in Scripture, opened my eyes to a new concept in the words of a favorite book, and calmed my worries as I journaled my prayers.

4. Attack (Practice the battle plan to take care of anxieties on the physical plane)

Paul tells us in Philippians 4:6, "Do not be anxious about anything, but in every situation, by prayer and petition, with thanksgiving, present your requests to God." Talk about a plan of attack!

Paul begins by saying, "Do not be anxious about anything."

He tells us to watch *how* we think about the things in our lives. It is with our thoughts we decide to believe the lies of the enemy, to be our own false prophets of the future, and steal our own happiness in life. Our thoughts give life or steal joy. We can live on purpose, according to the destiny God has set before us, or we can fall prey to the attack of the enemy and live life under a cloud of fear and worry.

Our thoughts give life or steal joy.

Paul goes on to say, "but in every situation ..."

We all have bad things happen in life, but it is our *thoughts* about the bad things that affect us. For me, it is true that Mark has a chronic illness that flares up at different times, but it is my thoughts that determine how I feel about the situation. When I am faced with an asthma flare-up, I can dissolve into my anxious "This is never going to get any better" mindset, or I can stand tall (with God's help) and speak truth, saying, "God, this is terrible, but I trust you are in control and will provide everything we need to walk through this. I trust you."

"Do not be anxious about anything, but in every situation, by prayer and petition, with thanksgiving, present your requests to God."

We attack by changing our thoughts and our behaviors. That's what I did that day. The tools of my attack were prayer and worship.

I prayed:

> *Help me not get stuck in unhealthy thoughts and behaviors.*
>
> *Help me not focus on myself and help me be brave for the family.*
>
> *Help me fight this fear that is on me so I can find your peace through this storm.*

I sang truth not because I felt like it, but because I made the decision to fight back. The truth is that God *is* my anchor. I am no longer a slave to fear. I am not alone. He is a good, good Father. And my prayer was for God to change my thoughts and my mindset, and that is what changed my behavior.

Now don't miss the fact that nothing about my circumstances had changed that day. Mark was still sick; we were still up to our eyeballs in medical bills and pharmaceutical needs; the boys were still worried and walking on eggshells wondering when Dad would be better, and we were still in crisis. But I broke down and begged God to help me. By prayer and petition, with thanksgiving (in my case, singing songs of worship), I made my requests to God.

Though my circumstances had not changed at all, I fought back against fear and against the tools of the enemy when I decided to worship in the middle of the storm.

> By worshiping, trusting, and praising God, you are telling the enemy loud and clear that you are not a woman to be messed with.

The enemy has a plan to keep us from experiencing the full life God has created for us. His plan counts on us being unaware and unarmed. To fight back, we must be aware of our thoughts and arm ourselves with the truth that Jesus spoke when he said, "In this world you will have trouble. But take heart! I have overcome the world" (John 16:33).

Action Steps

Check out page 208 for a list of the Four Good A's. You'll also find a link to print the Four Good A's to remind you of your battle plan.

- Ask God to open your eyes to unhealthy patterns of thought or behavior in your life.

- Have you ever had a breakdown that led to a breakthrough?
- What would life look like if you practiced the battle plan? Which of the Four A's do you need to practice more?

CHAPTER 4

WHAT IF THEY DON'T LIKE ME?

Fear of Rejection

In my third semester at the University of Tennessee, I signed up for an almost full schedule, but discovered I needed one more hour to be considered full-time. No one would have ever confused me with a star student, so instead of taking another challenging class, I went for an easy credit hour bowling. I had never bowled before, but bowling would bump me up to full-time status, and I thought it would be a fun way to meet new people on such a large campus.

On the first day of bowling class, my first opportunity to get to know my new classmates, I chose a cute baby-doll dress and some strappy flats. I mean, I wanted to make a good first impression, right? But as soon as I walked into the bowling alley, I knew I was in trouble. Clearly a dress was not the right choice! (Can you say wardrobe malfunction?)

The course instructor gave us a few simple instructions and then told us to trade in our shoes and select a ball. Trade in my shoes? What in the world? (I really had never bowled before.) The idea of putting my bare feet into shoes that other people had worn was a little too much for me. But I managed to get past that, selected my ball, and headed for my assigned lane.

There were just so many things I had to get over in order to bowl. I told myself, "Alright, Alli, you can do this. Don't think about these gross shoes. Don't bend over too far in this stupid dress. Just put your fingers in the ball, walk up to the lane, and throw it. Little kids do this. Easy."

When it was my turn to bowl, I held the heavy ball in my hand and mentally rehearsed the steps I would take and the spectacular way I would release the ball.

I stepped too far out onto the slippery waxed lane and lifted the ball back just as I'd seen the others do. Unlike them, though, I started to lose my balance. Panicking, I gripped the ball with superhuman strength, and instead of releasing the ball, I did a 180, guided by the weight of the ball that was still in my death grip. You know what happened next. I fell, butt first, legs out, right in front of all my classmates. Humiliated, I scrambled to pull my dress down, stood up, cracked a joke, and took an overly dramatic bow.

Everyone, of course, roared with laughter, and so did I. I sat back down with my classmates and laughed. We all laughed for the rest of the class, but inside I was still dying from embarrassment.

I wasn't about to let everybody see how horrified I really was.

After class, I was in a bathroom stall when some of the girls (not realizing I was in there) came in talking about the class and, to my horror, my great bowling adventure. These girls weren't like me. They were classy girls, the kind with straight, smooth hair, who never ate any carbs and probably never worried about fitting in. Me? I was insecure with crazy, curly, unruly hair, always trying to fit in, and somehow always managing to embarrass myself in the worst possible way.

One of the girls said, "That girl is such a spaz. What is wrong with her? And who wears a dress to go bowling?"

Pulling my feet up so they wouldn't notice me, I held my breath. I stayed in the bathroom stall until they were all gone, and then I stayed there longer to make sure that they had left the building.

For the rest of the day I huddled in the comfort of my steel dorm-room bed, eating ice cream (hello, bingeing!) and feeling sorry for myself. Sure, I was humiliated from falling down and making a fool of myself, but I could have survived that. The ridicule from the girls in the restroom was too much to take. Thank the Lord this happened before social media blew up, or it would have been all over Instagram!

I never went back to that class again. I couldn't handle the rejection I felt or the pain that came with it. And no way was I going to give those girls an opportunity to reject me again! Of course, at the end of the semester, I had a hard time explaining to my mom why I had an incomplete in a bowling class that was supposed to be an easy credit hour.

Fear tells us to reject and protect.

Faith tells us to forgive and accept.

Looking back, I can see that by not returning to that class, I was trying to protect myself. I was rejecting my classmates (at my own expense) before they could reject me again. Experts say this is classic behavior when it comes to rejection: reject before you get rejected.

Pecked to Death

Rejection is like death by a thousand cuts. As Guy Winch writes in *Emotional First Aid: Healing Rejection, Guilt, Failure, and Other Everyday Hurts*, "Rejection elicits emotional pain so sharp, it affects our thinking, floods us with anger, erodes our confidence and self-esteem, and destabilizes our fundamental feeling of belonging."[1] That pretty much sums it all up perfectly right there, doesn't it?

Rejection pierces us in our most vulnerable places, the deepest parts of our hearts and minds, and creates in us a fear that is just as deep as the rejection itself. The fear of rejection can come from a single traumatic event, like a close friend ending a friendship, or it can come from situations like my overhearing the cool girls' conversation in the bathroom.

But the fear of rejection can also be triggered by small everyday events, like your child not getting invited to a birthday party or your coworkers going to lunch without you. As my mom used to say, "Rejection is like being pecked to death by chickens. One little peck doesn't do that much damage, but when they peck you over and over, it all adds up." One little hurt, after another little hurt, after another little hurt, until you walk around full of little wounds just waiting for someone else to reject you.

If we aren't careful and we allow the fear of rejection to dominate our lives, it will suck the life right out of us.

How Rejection Steals Our Joy

1. We get stuck

Let's face it, when we feel rejected, logic goes out the window, and we don't think clearly. Before long we find ourselves spiraling downward into a whirlpool of negativity, saying things like this to ourselves:

- "They don't like me as much as I thought they did."
- "They'll never like me."
- "I'm a failure."
- "It feels like I'm invisible."
- "No one really likes me."
- "I'm not good enough."

When we have this downward spiral of thoughts, we get stuck in a vicious cycle that grows stronger the longer we let it continue, until eventually it leaves us feeling hopeless. We imagine the worst, and we get stuck.

2. We avoid situations where there's any possibility for a rejection or hurt

Looking back, I feel silly that I made an incomplete in bowling all because I assumed everyone thought the same thing as those cool girls in the bathroom. Rather than risk being rejected or hurt again, I avoided the whole situation. Not only did it cost me the extra tuition, but it also cost me the extra time it took to replace that class with another one. Like I said, when we feel rejected, we aren't always thinking logically, and we tend to avoid any situation where the hurt could happen again.

3. We overgeneralize

After thirteen years of marriage and three beautiful children (all under age ten), Anne's husband told her he didn't love her anymore and that he had fallen in love with another woman. Anne told herself that she would never let herself be hurt like that again, so she shut down the part of her heart that would allow herself to love another man. Instead, she busied herself with work and raising her children (both legitimate responsibilities), and she avoided any and all social situations where she could potentially meet (or be set up with) another life mate. Eventually, friends stopped inviting Anne because they knew her answer would be no, which in turn only confirmed to Anne's heart that she was unlovable. Talk about stealing joy!

We all have a tendency to overgeneralize situations. We come to a conclusion based on one experience (or some negative trigger from our past), and we apply it to all future experiences. In fact, experts say that overgeneralization[2] is one of the most common distortions in our thinking. And the more situations cause us pain, the more likely we are to overgeneralize that pain and see the world through that lens of hurt.

Overgeneralization is especially dangerous when we look at

life through the lens of hearts that have been wounded by rejection. We see all relationships as potential minefields of hurt, and we see ourselves as fundamentally unworthy and rejected.

Everyday Rejections

As I mentioned earlier, everyday rejections can be the biggest joy thieves of all. It's those little slights that seem to do the most damage. You know the ones I'm talking about:

- Neighbors don't invite us to their cookouts.
- We learn at church that the mom's group had a play date and we didn't know a thing about it.
- Our friends go out to dinner with another set of friends, and we wonder why we didn't get invited.
- Or we get invited to something last minute, but we have the feeling that we were more of an oversight than anything else.

All of these scenarios, mundane as they are, cause us real pain. In fact, research shows the same areas in our brains that register physical harm also register the hurt and pain we feel from rejection.[3] Our brain responds to our hearts being hurt and the pain of our emotional wounds, just like it responds to pain and hurt from physical wounds. In other words, we actually "feel" emotional pain the same way we feel physical pain.

For some, the greatest source of everyday rejection is a phenomenon called "social media rejection."

The problem with the Internet is we see everything: every friend's dinner, every comment our friends make on other people's posts, every party as it happens in real time, every time our friends go for a walk or a picnic. It's all photographed, filtered, captioned, and up for the world to see.

We don't often talk about what we feel when we are left out, rejected by, or forgotten on social media, but we should recognize it and acknowledge it, because we aren't going to stop using Instagram, Facebook, and all the rest anytime soon. Although I know as a moderately well-adjusted adult that I shouldn't feel rejected when I see situations where people are out having fun and I wasn't invited, I still feel hurt. Pretending like it doesn't hurt doesn't help me deal with it or heal from it.

Some examples from social media that leave people feeling rejected are:

- Seeing a photo on Facebook of friends all out together at a social gathering that you didn't know about.
- Commenting on a friend's post and feeling like the comment was ignored while everyone else is commenting back and forth.
- Posting a picture of a very important life event and our closest friends don't comment or even like it.

I have a friend, Dawn, who is part of a brand new church. She and her launch team had worked hard all day transforming an elementary school into what would be their church on Sundays. It was backbreaking work, but at the same time one of the most rewarding things she'd ever been a part of.

As she and her husband and the rest of the team left that day, they were all hugging and happy and excited about the launch that would happen the next morning. She ran back in to grab something in the building while everyone else said their goodbyes. When she hopped in her car several minutes later, she was as happy as she could be . . . until she got on Facebook and saw a picture of the entire launch team (posing in front of the building and their new church sign). There was a big empty spot right next to her husband. The caption said, "Many thanks to this incredible group of men and women who have worked tirelessly to make this dream a reality."

She was so hurt and angry because no one realized she was missing from the picture. All the joy and excitement she felt over the start of their new church was crushed from *one picture* she saw on social media.

Another upsetting aspect of social media is that people tend to do things they wouldn't do if they were face-to-face with someone. For example, if I were at a picnic and someone said something I disagreed with, I wouldn't stop being friends with that person. I would probably just excuse myself and go get another piece of fried chicken. But on Facebook, if someone goes on and on about some controversial topic (like an angry, name-calling political rant, for example), it is not uncommon at all for people to just unfollow the person. And by the very nature of social media, these cut-offs happen often, yet feel much harsher than just excusing ourselves from the picnic table.

Having a friend unfriend or unfollow us doesn't mean that friend doesn't love us; maybe it really just means the friend doesn't want to see political updates or sweaty after-gym pictures on Facebook every day. However, in the moment, the rejection hurts just like physical pain to our brains, and we feel terrible.

We have so many ways that our feelings get hurt thanks to modern technology. On the Internet, we can feel rejected by potentially thousands of people (yay!).

The Ultimate Rejection

It's difficult feeling rejected by our friends or even our acquaintances on the Internet (that sounds funny when I think about it, but hey, it's the world we live in), but can you imagine what it would feel like to be rejected by twelve of your closest friends?

Jesus, God incarnate, came to earth as a man. He was all God, yet all human. He knew our joys, our sorrows, our struggles, and our pain. And he felt the sting of rejection.

In the moments leading up to his death on the cross, almost everyone in Jesus's life had rejected him. It started with Judas betraying him to the soldiers in the garden, and culminated with Jesus's outcry to his own Father from the cross, "My God, my God, why have you forsaken me?" (Mark 15:34).

But no discussion of Jesus's rejection would be complete without talking about his close friend and disciple Peter. Personally, I love Peter. I connect with him. He was excitable, ran his mouth too much, and was always messing up. Yet despite all Peter's weaknesses, long before he was even stable or mature, God still chose him to preach and lay the foundation for the early church. (Don't you just love that about God?)

Peter was one of Jesus's closest friends; he was there from the beginning of Jesus's earthly ministry; he witnessed the miracles; he was the first to recognize Jesus as the Christ; he saw him transfigured (while running his mouth, of course!), and he even briefly walked on water with Jesus. But you know what the kicker is here? After all that, after all of those amazing experiences, he still rejected Jesus. Not once, not twice, but *three* times.

The worst example of Peter's denial of Jesus occurred after Jesus was arrested, and Peter was recognized as being a follower of Jesus.

About an hour later, another person spoke up. "This fellow must have been with Jesus," he said. "He is from Galilee." Peter replied, "Man, I don't know what you're talking about!"

Just as he was speaking, the rooster crowed. The Lord turned and looked right at Peter. Then Peter remembered what the Lord had spoken to him. "The rooster will crow today," Jesus had said. "Before it does, you will say three times that you don't know me." Peter went outside. He broke down and sobbed. (Luke 22:59–62)

Jesus knows the pain of being abandoned, the gut punch of having your closest friends betray you. As Isaiah 53:3 says, "He was despised and rejected by mankind, a man of suffering, and familiar with pain."

Peter's rejection didn't lessen who Jesus was. Jesus knew what Peter (and the rest of the disciples, and even the whole Jewish community) would do, and he didn't take it personally or question his calling. Jesus never thought, "Well, if Peter of all people rejected me after all this, maybe I'm not God enough to be the Messiah."

Now I'm sure you're thinking, *Well, of course Jesus didn't let rejection stop him from fulfilling his purpose. He's God.* Yes, as God, Jesus turned water into wine, raised the dead to life, and turned one tuna fish sandwich into enough to feed the masses. We don't expect ourselves to do those things. But Jesus was also human. And there are lots of things that Jesus did, that Jesus modeled, that we should strive to emulate.

Jesus's love for others, his kindness, his compassion, his laser focus on his calling—these are all traits that as believers and followers of Jesus we want to emulate. I believe that Jesus not getting sidetracked by the pain of rejection is an important lesson for us all. Like Jesus, we may feel the pain of rejection, but we can also know that we are loved and called by name to a destiny set out before us. The gut-punch of rejection can not and *should not* take that knowledge from us.

Because he was human, Jesus understands our pain and understands exactly what we're going through when we feel rejected. He is with us in the pain, and although he may not deliver us from the hurt of rejection, he will give us strength to go through it.

And the most reassuring thing about Jesus is that *he will never reject us*. The Bible tells us his love for us is never failing and unceasing. As it says in Romans 8:38–39, "For I am convinced that neither death nor life, neither angels nor demons, neither the present nor the future, nor any powers, neither height nor depth, nor anything else in all creation, will be able to separate us from the love of God that is in Christ Jesus our Lord."

> **Although Jesus may not deliver us from the pain of rejection, he will give us strength to go through it.**

Having a rock-solid assurance of Jesus's love for us is crucial for enduring the pain of rejection.

A Battle Plan to Fight the Fear of Rejection

When I face the fear of rejection, I rely on some easy-to-use strategies to fight back.

1. Play the *So What?* Game

Understanding that it's normal to feel rejected can be super helpful on its own. But to really overcome the fear of rejection, we have to learn fight the fear. One of the ways I like to fight fear is by playing what I call the *So What?* Game."

As a young teenager I had a lot of anxiety, most of which was rooted in losing my dad as a child. Eventually, my mom, wise woman that she is, suggested that I might need to talk things out with a professional. I loved Pamela, my counselor. She made me feel like no topic was off limits and often encouraged me to just let it all out. After I would finish a tirade about how terrible a potential situation was, she would ask, "So what?"

Initially I was annoyed by the seemingly rude and simplistic question. *"So what?"* I repeated back to her in my sassy teenage way, "What do you mean, *so what?*"

"So what if that happened? Would it be the end of the world? "Well, no. The world wouldn't end." (Dramatic teenage sigh.) "Would you actually die?"

"Noooooo." (Can you picture me rolling my eyes?)

Pamela: "Okay, so what would you do next?"

She made me question my anxious thoughts one by one, until I had worked through every possible scenario in my head, especially the imaginary worst-case scenarios. Even today, the act of working out all my *what-if* scenarios allows me to identify the thoughts that aren't realistic and look at them from a new perspective.

2. Use truth talk

I had to learn to look at situations that made me feel afraid and worried and ask myself, "So what?" Once I walked through the *so what?* exercise, I learned that I also had to do some truth talk, replacing the worst-case scenario with a statement of truth. For example, had I used the so-what exercise and the truth talk technique for the bowling class situation, I would have told myself this:

- "I can't go back to that class. Those girls might make fun of me again." So what?
- "I'll be embarrassed and probably will never be able to bowl right." So what?
- "I might fail the class if I don't learn to bowl." So what?

You get the picture.

And here's what my truth talk would have looked like:

- "I can go back to class. It's not going to be the end of the world."
- "I will probably laugh it off with a few people, and those people will end up becoming my friends."

- "If I keep showing up to class, I'll eventually learn how to bowl well enough to pass."

Using truth talk to replace our anxious, fearful thoughts with truth is a great way to fight back against the fear that paralyzes us.

3. Plan how to cope

Finally, once you have asked, "So what?" and you have done some truth talk, the last step is to plan out three ways you can cope, even if rejection happens.

For example, how could I have coped if the girls had made fun of me again? I could have talked to the teacher after class and asked to be put on another lane (it was a big class, after all). And what if I was embarrassed and had a hard time bowling? I could try to enjoy the people around me and be light-hearted about my less-than-pro skills as a bowler.

Learning to fight fear by asking, "So what?" then doing a little truth talk, and finally listing out ways to cope has been so helpful for times when I feel my anxiety building because of the fear of rejection.

But how do we recover when we have actually felt the pain of rejection and unacceptance from others?

How to Recover When We Feel Rejected

Since our brain does not distinguish whether the pain we feel is from a physical hurt or an emotional hurt, we need to be good to ourselves and practice emotional self-care. Just as we take care of our physical bodies when we hurt, we need to take care of our hearts when we feel the pain of rejection. Here are five ways to cushion the blow and comfort ourselves when our hearts feel rejected.

1. Don't assume that the rejection is personal

Laura's son Derek was not invited to the birthday party of his close friend who also happened to be their next-door neighbor. Laura, upset and feeling that her son had been personally rejected, told her husband, "I just don't think she likes me, and she's taking it out on him." A couple of days later, the neighbor told Laura, "Hey, the girls really wanted to have their birthday party at that silly hair and makeup party place this year. I knew Derek wouldn't want to come to that, so we are going to invite you guys to our smaller family party the next day." Laura had assumed the rejection was personal, but in truth, it wasn't a rejection at all.

Sometimes we *are* left out, but even then, the oversight might not be personal. I often say, "Not everyone can be invited to everything. And that should be okay. We aren't in high school!" (Sometimes I say that as a pep talk to myself!)

2. Ban negative self-talk

When we feel rejected, we shouldn't take it out on ourselves. It's too easy to kick ourselves when we are already down. If we aren't careful we can take rejection from others to heart and start a pattern of self-rejection through negative self-talk.

When we feel hurt, we have a tendency to make matters worse because we talk to ourselves in a negative way. The voice in our head is often negative and critical, saying things like, "I shouldn't feel this way," or "I'm so stupid," or some other negative comment.

Self-criticism is often confused with humility, but it's not; it's straight-up sinful behavior. If Jesus doesn't talk to us that way, why do we think it's okay to be so mean to ourselves? When you catch yourself being self-critical and self-rejecting, you have to repent and pray that Jesus will help you see yourself the way he sees you and that you will treat yourself the way he wants you treated.

It's okay to be sad, and it's okay to be frustrated. When we believe the lie that we shouldn't feel our negative feelings, it puts us in a spiral of self-loathing. Give yourself permission to feel your emotions, accept them, and then the healing can come.

Rejection can feel like a loss or a death. When we lose something, it does hurt. Beating ourselves up and telling ourselves that we *should* feel a different way only makes things worse.

3. Remember how Jesus sees you

Reassurance from other people will never be enough until we know we are loved and valued by God. God made this promise to his people, the Israelites, and repeated it again to believers in Jesus: "Never will I leave you. Never will I forsake you" (Deuteronomy 31:6, 8; Hebrews 13:5). What a comfort!

Jesus, by his very nature, will never and can never reject us. People may hurt our feelings, leave us out, or even break our hearts, but Jesus loves us, accepts us, and will never leave us. Before he left the earth, he reassured us, "Surely I am with you always, to the very end of the age" (Matthew 28:20).

> Rejection reinforces our deepest fear— that we aren't enough.

Once we dig in and understand how Jesus sees us and *stays* with us, we can live lives secure in his love. We can grow from self-rejection to self-compassion.

4. Connect with people who care about you

When we feel rejected, we don't feel like we belong. Rejection's pain is especially painful because it touches on our deepest fear triggers of, "Am I good enough? Am I worth loving?"

We have to get that deep sense of belonging back, first by connecting to Jesus, then by connecting with others. Our close friends or family members often provide the reality check we need, reminding us that we are loved, that we are accepted, and that we belong. Having good friends that you can visit or talk to at a moment's notice restores our need for connection.

I can't tell you how many times I have called my friend Carol on a rant about how I feel rejected by something or someone, and after I pour out my heart she will calmly say, "You know that has nothing to do with you and you're being hyper-sensitive, right?" In my gut, I knew it all along, but I needed the reminder that I was blowing it out of proportion.

5. Ask yourself, "What would I tell my best friend?"

When we feel pain, we tend to take a negative outlook on things, brooding over worst-case scenarios in our head. But if we get a little distance from our pain, we will be able to see it more clearly. If your best friend came to you and told you about the situation, what would your encouragement to her be? Because when it's a friend's pain and not our own, we're less likely to overgeneralize or blow things out of proportion.

The enemy uses our fear against us, taking our most precious thing and convincing us we will lose it. As we learn to fight our fears, especially the fear of rejection, we become better equipped to deal with that fear and learn not to let it keep us from living our lives with joy and purpose.

Action Steps

Turn to page 209 for a space that you can use to fight back against the fear of rejection by using "Truth Talk."

- When do you first remember feeling rejected? Ask God to heal those places in your heart that the fear of rejection still lives in.
- Think about how social media has fed into feelings of

rejection. How can you use the fear of rejection battle plan to fight these feelings?

- When you are feeling rejected or afraid of rejection, ask yourself what three things you know to be true even in that moment.
- Identify one or two people with whom you can be vulnerable about your feelings and fear of rejection when the triggers pop up. Nurture those relationships, because they are key to fighting back against rejection.

CHAPTER 5

WHAT IF THE KIDS AREN'T OKAY?

Fear for Our Children

When my first son was born, I became an instant expert on everything that could possibly go wrong with a little baby. For me, there was nothing scarier than realizing I was responsible for another human being, a tiny vulnerable little person that didn't even come with an instruction manual. Not only did I have to grow this human being in my body (talk about fear of failure), I also had to raise this human to become a functioning, well-adjusted adult. I don't care if you are a flaming-sword-swallowing tightrope walker or a former Navy Seal, that kind of responsibility is flat-out terrifying.

Fortunately for me (and for little Justin), my pregnancy and early years of parenting came about before the Internet was particularly useful. I had plenty of worries of my own without piling on extra fear thanks to Google. If blogs and parenting forums had been around when Justin was born, I may very well have driven myself crazy googling all the things I worried about.

During pregnancy I worried if I was eating enough, resting enough, and taking the right prenatal vitamins. When he was a newborn, I worried if he was swaddled tight enough to feel secure. If not, would he always feel insecure and unloved because he flopped around, startling himself with those wild newborn baby arm flops?

Or was he swaddled so tightly that his hands would lose blood flow and his fingers would never work properly, completely destroying any chance he had at being an accomplished artist, pro athlete, or break dancer?

What if he grew up and had a strange fear of cows because we put him under a mobile of farm animals?

There were so many ways I could mess up my baby and do this parenting thing wrong, it wasn't even funny (though it seems hilarious now).

I worried about air pollution, what I ate while breastfeeding him, what number of baths he should have per week, and most of all I worried he was going to stop breathing in the middle the night. He didn't have any breathing problems and there were no indications that this would be an issue, but that didn't stop me from worrying one tiny bit. I obsessed. That precious, seven-pound baby boy was out in the world, and the thought that he might stop breathing drove me into a state of inescapable fear.

So of course, lacking the help of Google and crowdsourcing wisdom from the collective Internet, I did what any fearful mama with disposable income does. I went shopping. I bought a little electric sensor for under his crib mattress that was designed to buzz like ten firetruck alarms if he ever stopped breathing. In my mind, I imagined the ten firetruck alarms going off, and I would rush to his crib and perform magic baby CPR to make him start breathing again. (Of course, I didn't actually know magic baby CPR, or any CPR for that matter.) I was a woman on a mission.

The comfort of knowing an alarm would sound if my precious baby boy stopped breathing put my worried mama heart at rest. At least it was comforting for a few hours that first night. The problem wasn't that the sensor didn't work; the problem was we didn't always remember when we needed to turn it off. In the middle of the night, when Justin cried, we wandered into his nursery, half-asleep, picked him up, and carried him to our bed. Just as we lay down in our bed and got all comfy with him, that ten firetruck alarm started shrieking. It's a miracle we didn't toss Justin out of bed the way we fought those covers to get to the shut-off button on that alarm!

And I'd love to tell you that only happened one time, but unfortunately, as half-asleep parents, we rarely remembered to turn off the stupid sensor.

The fear of Sudden Infant Death Syndrome is nothing to sneeze at. Nothing could be more terrifying than the idea that you could lose your baby while you're sleeping. But I was so afraid of SIDS that I essentially booby-trapped the nursery and drove Mark and me crazy.

But fear does that when it comes to our children, doesn't it?

Parenthood is like entering a fear marathon that never ends.

A Million *What-Ifs*

The fear that something will happen to our children, the worry that they will get hurt, and the anxiety that we can't protect them from harm is enough to turn the most confident parent into a big, massive pile of raw nerves. We play out a million *what-ifs* in our head from the time we learn we are pregnant until the day they leave our home (and long after that, from what I'm told).

If pregnancy and infancy don't leave us curled up in the fetal position out of fear, then we have to will ourselves to survive the fears of the toddler and preschool years (because well, c'mon, toddlers are little savages, bless them!). We secretly fear we are terrible moms because our kid doesn't measure up to the other kids in the playgroup, and we fear they'll never be potty trained and will wind up in kindergarten in a diaper. (Don't laugh, this is a legit fear!)

Then it's on to the school years, when we worry our kids aren't as smart as other kids, or they won't fit in with other children. We worry they aren't getting enough extracurricular activities to be a well-rounded person, that they aren't great at sports, or that they don't even know what a Suzuki violin is, much less how to play it. We fear they aren't truly happy, they will fall in with the wrong crowd, they will make bad decisions, they will text and drive, they will fall in love with the wrong person, and the list goes on and on and on. (I feel a little anxious just writing all these out.)

Your worries won't change your *what-ifs*, but prayer will.

From small, fleeting fears to the ones that keep us up at night, these *what-ifs* make our stomachs tight with worry and drive us to our knees in prayer.

Sometimes, though, we walk around with daily fear and anxiety about our kids, and we don't even realize it is there. All we know is we're tense and stressed out.

This happened to a good friend of mine. She wrote to me and said she never realized how much fear she had about her kids until I started talking about fear as I tackled this book. (I'm a blast at parties now. "Hi, friends, let's talk about your deep dark fears!") She wrote to me, "They are so vulnerable (physically, emotionally, and spiritually) that when I picture them going through life, the world suddenly seems to be a very dark and dangerous place. What if someone kidnaps them? Molests them? Runs them over? Bullies them? Peer pressures them into destructive behaviors? And what about their own intrinsic tendency to rebel against God, give in to sin, cause harm to themselves and others? And just freak accidents that could happen to them when I'm not looking?"

Wouldn't it be great if the Bible had a whole book on exactly how to parent well, a book that we could turn to when the *what-ifs* threatened to overwhelm us?

We could look into Parenting 2:14, for example, and find out if we really have to feed our children organic baby food.

Or maybe in Parenting 4:3 we could learn how much screen time is appropriate for a three-year-old.

We could even flip over to Parenting 24:2 and find out what a sixteen-year-old's curfew should be.

I'd really love to find the part in Parenting 35:7 that says when your children act like jerks it's totally not your fault. But when they are angels, you are to receive all the credit. Amen!

But, of course, we know the Bible is not written like that. The world is ever changing, and God wasn't overly concerned with giving us the ABCs and 123s of parenthood. He didn't give us a how-to manual. He gave us some basic principles and the Holy Spirit to guide us. But to truly trust the Holy Spirit's leading, we have to emotionally and spiritually let our children go and trust them wholeheartedly to the Lord—and that's absolutely easier said than done.

Letting Go

If ever there was a mom who understood about letting her child go and trusting God, it was Jochebed, the mother of Moses.

In the first chapter of the book of Exodus, we read that the Israelites had so outnumbered the Egyptians, Pharaoh feared the Israelites would someday revolt against him. Because of his fear, he ordered the Hebrew midwives to put to death any new-born males. But the midwives feared God more than they feared Pharaoh, so they disobeyed his cruel order. When Pharaoh realized his orders had been disobeyed, he ordered his armies to go into the Israelites' homes and drown all their male children in the Nile River.

In Exodus 2:1–2 we read, "Now a man from the house of Levi

went and married a daughter of Levi. The woman conceived and bore a son; and when she saw that he was beautiful, she hid him for three months."

I cannot even imagine the terror Jochebed must have endured for those three months that she held that sweet baby in her arms, knowing that death was literally waiting outside the door of her home. I imagine she must have been trying to come up with a thousand different scenarios on how to save Moses from the Egyptians. She knew if she did not do something, his life would end.

The story goes on to say,

> But when she could hide him no longer, she got him a wicker basket and covered it over with tar and pitch. Then she put the child into it and set it among the reeds by the bank of the Nile. The daughter of Pharaoh came down to bathe at the Nile, with her maidens walking alongside the Nile; and she saw the basket among the reeds and sent her maid, and she brought it to her. When she opened it, she saw the child, and behold, the boy was crying. And she had pity on him and said, "This is one of the Hebrews' children." (Exodus 2:3–6)

Moses's sister, Miriam, who was hiding in the reeds, offered to take Moses to a Hebrew women to be nursed—a Hebrew woman who just *happened* to be Jochebed. Moses was raised by his own mother until he was old enough to go and live in the palace with the princess (but that part of the story is for another lesson).

Jochebed was a wise woman. She had carefully made the bottom of Moses's basket waterproof, she chose just the right location (where I believe she knew the Pharaoh's daughter bathed each day), and then she placed that basket in the river.

I can only imagine the death grip she had on that basket, but then she did what so many of us find impossible to do. She released her baby and his future into the hands of God.

Jochebed couldn't have known what God would do in the life of her baby boy. She had no way of knowing Moses would someday be used by God to free the Hebrew people. All she knew was she had to release him into God's care.

Sometimes, as parents, we must do the very best we can do, and then we must release our children into God's care, trusting that his plan for them is better than ours. I'm not saying it is easy to do. It isn't. I have held onto the reins of control over my children enough times to know surrender isn't easy.

When our children stop living under our constant watchful eye, from the first day of preschool to the first time behind the wheel of the car to the day they step out of the home as adults, our fear for them can become debilitating.

God's care is better than our control.

There comes a point in our lives when we are forced into that moment of surrender.

In that moment we have to say, "God, I know you love this child more than I do; it's why I'm surrendering and trusting you with them." And then we have to push that basket out into the river.

Sometimes, though, we are so overcome by our fear for our children, we simply can't let go.

Because, we know how real that fear is, we know we must have a battle plan to combat that fear.

A Battle Plan to Fight Our Fear for Our Children

Fear for our children is visceral, primeval, and sometimes pervasive. If we don't get a grip on it ASAP, it could end up ruling our lives (and perhaps ruining theirs—hello, helicopter parenting). Here are my best tips and tricks for tackling the mother of all fears: fear for our children.

1. Determine if the fear is real or perceived

Fear is often an irrational response to an uncertain set of circumstances. And, as we've already learned, our brains do not understand the difference between real and perceived fear. Our body responds exactly the same way. We panic.

When I was pregnant with one of my sons, I watched a segment on TV about a father and son team who competed in races, including the Ironman triathlon. What made this father and son team so special was the son competed from his wheelchair with his father pushing him. The son was born with cerebral palsy because the umbilical cord wrapped around his neck in utero and restricted the flow of oxygen to his brain.

Of course, I cried like a baby during this touching story, then became immediately obsessed with the fear that the umbilical cord would wrap around my own baby's neck. There were no signs that my baby wasn't moving as much as he normally did, but I was a frazzled, nervous wreck and all but demanded my doctor perform an ultrasound. I couldn't eat, I couldn't sleep, and until I saw the ultrasound for myself, I worried that my baby's brain was being deprived of oxygen. My fear was totally perceived, but it surely felt real.

There are times as a mom when I become freaked out about something, and I have to ask myself, "Is this something real that's likely to happen, or is this something that I'm just worried about?"

Is this something real that's likely to happen, or is this something that I'm just worried about?

If it's real, I know that I must be wise, make a plan of action, and then rest in the assurance that I can trust God. For example, I have a friend whose daughter had something serious going on with her vision. She couldn't get the school administrators to listen to her about her concerns because her daughter had passed the school's vision screening. Not sure about whether to take her daughter to the doctor or not, she asked "Dr. Google" what he thought about the symptoms. By the end of her research, she felt certain her daughter had a brain tumor. (P.S. Google is not a good way to diagnose anything!) But instead of sitting around panicking and believing the worst, she took her daughter to the doctor. There she discovered her daughter had a very fixable vision problem that could be remedied with therapy and prescriptive glasses. Hooray, easy fix! Hooray, not living in fear!

If the fear is perceived, then I give myself a pep talk: *Alli, this isn't real. You are imagining the worst-case scenario, and you are working yourself up into a worry storm. Calm it down, girl.*

Surprisingly, just telling myself (and my overactive imagination) that it's not real works! Sometimes I have to tell myself multiple times, but the more I reassure myself that my fears are unfounded, the better I am able to relax and release my fear.

2. Determine the level of control you have over the situation

The second step in battling the fears over our children is to ask ourselves realistically what level of control we have over the situation. Fear can make us tighten the grip of control over our family and the details of our lives to such an unhealthy degree that we squeeze out all the life and enjoyment from it.

Our oldest son is a great driver. He drives my car, which is an absolute tank, but I still have to talk myself off the proverbial ledge when he is driving without me. When I know he is behind the wheel of a car, if I hear the wail of a siren, my stomach ties up in knots and I fear that something has happened to him.

When he first got his license, I never wanted him to drive anywhere. And if he did drive anywhere, I had a list of rules twelve miles long related to his driving. I might not be in the car with him, but I made sure I controlled every ounce of the situation that I could control. Although he had never given me a reason to doubt his driving skills, I was squeezing the life out of the poor boy and making him fearful of driving.

I was talking to one of my oldest friends recently, the kind of friend who knows the good, the bad, and the ugly and manages to love me anyway. She asked me if I thought the reason I was so obsessively fearful of Justin having an accident was because my father passed away in a car accident when he was only twenty-three years old. She loved me enough to gently confront me about my excessive fear and controlling tendencies when it came to my son's driving.

At first I told her no and that she was crazy, but after a while I had to admit that she knew what she was talking about. Growing up with that huge loss created a fear trigger inside me. I'm afraid, at a gut level, of losing the ones I love most that same way.

What I have come to understand is that my fear of Justin getting hurt behind the wheel of a car is real (he's a teenage boy), and it's perceived (based on circumstances from my past). There is some level of control I do have, like how many friends he can have in the car and where he can go in my car, but there are other things, like other drivers on the road, that I have no control over. I know my son is a responsible driver, and he is as safe as any other driver out there on the road. I have to fight the urge to try and clamp down control on him, and instead allow him to grow up and exist in the world outside of my control.

I have had to learn to say, "I don't know what's outside that door. But, Lord, I release him to you."

Also, as a parent, I have battled crazy amounts of fear that something would happen to me and I would leave my family without a mom. With every flight that took off and every annual physical, all the potential ways for me to meet my demise would go through my mind.

I had to accept that I could only do so much. I wear my seat belt, go to the doctor, and take my vitamins, but my future, and the future of my children, is in God's hands. He knows the number of our days, and nothing I do will change that. He's set out a bright future in front of our children, and we have to learn to take a breath, give it to God, and trust his plans for us.

When we become aware of our fears and determine if they are real or perceived and decide what we can and cannot (or should not) control—then the extreme anxiety we feel because of the fear is lessened.

3. Don't feed the fears

I am not a fan of scary movies at all. I can easily translate unrealistic events from scary movies into real-life scenarios, especially if I am home alone at night. (And I still, as a thirty-nine-year-old woman, won't hang my hand over the side of the bed . . . that's just tempting a monster to grab it!) So guess what? I don't watch scary movies. Why in the world would I want to feed those fears?

The same is true of fears related to my kids. We live in a culture that tells us to be afraid for our children, that impending danger is around every corner. Twenty-four-hour news gives us a constant supply of new things to worry about. Every time I turn on the news, I hear stories about a toddler being snatched up by an alligator or gorilla, or a deadly virus that could come to the US, or a report about how it will cost me roughly six million dollars to raise a child (and then I multiply that times *five!*).

I recently realized that the more TV news I watched, the more fearful I became about remote and disastrous scenarios happening to my children. Brooding over what might happen, based on what I was seeing in the news, turned me into a crazy woman. I obsessed about how to keep my kids from getting bit by mosquitoes, or abducted by strangers, or any of the other horrible things I saw on cable TV. While I wanted to be aware of what was happening in the world, I knew I could not continue to feed my parenting fears by watching the news.

I managed the input I gave my brain by reading news on an app once a day, quickly, instead of turning on cable news. This way I stayed informed, but I wasn't "over-informed," and I didn't feed my fears.

Perhaps you feed your fears in other ways. Maybe you:

- Obsessively Google every symptom or problem you observe in your child.
- Let yourself be influenced by the fears of anxious friends.
- Talk too much about your fears because it gets you sympathy and attention. (Not that I know anything about that. Ahem.)

Learning to manage the flow of information and the behaviors that amplify your fears for your children is an important part of your battle plan.

4. Lean on your battle buddies

A friend once told me that in the Army, battle buddies are peers who assist each other in and out of combat. They look after each other's physical and mental health.

As moms, I think we need battle buddies to help us battle through the onslaught of fear and worry that comes at us. We need battle buddy moms who have kids in the same stages as ours, as well as battle buddies who are a little farther along and can walk with us and offer wise counsel.

Very often, especially as moms, we don't share our parenting fears because we want people to think we have it all together. Having authentic relationships that allow you to be transparent and vulnerable are critical to keeping your parenting fears from consuming you. It's important to have other people you can lean on, fellow parents with whom you can share your fears, moms that will help talk you through the tough times without allowing you to wallow in your fears.

Of course, you want to be careful that your battle buddies are people you *can* lean on. You don't want someone who will feed your fears by indulging them or expanding on them, but you also don't want someone who will make you feel insecure for having them. Instead, you want a battle buddy who will listen to your fears *up to a point*, then help you get some perspective on the situation.

When we lived in Maryland fourteen years ago, I was still an overly hovering mom to only two little guys (now teenagers), and my battle buddy was Missy, a fun-loving mom of five. She was about ten years ahead of me with her kids, and I watched in awe as she managed her large family but somehow didn't let the chaos of the five kids drive her crazy.

I used to share all my parenting fears about my two-and four-year-old, and she would listen nicely and give great advice. I never felt judged for cutting my boys' grapes in quarters, or for bathing them in hand sanitizer every time they touched anything.

I used to wonder how Missy could be so calm with all those kids, and now that I have five kids, I know she probably realized she was outnumbered and that control was futile by kid number three. There's something liberating about the realization that your kids are individuals, on a path set before them by God, and there's only so much control you have. We can either hold on to the illusion of control and believe the lie that we are 100 percent responsible for every success or failure in their lives, or we can live in the freedom that we know we are just stewards for a short time and we might as well enjoy it along the way.

Missy, my battle buddy from years ago, taught me how to enjoy motherhood while fighting the daily worries that inevitably pop up. Think about the moms who share this journey with you. Are they helpful allies, or do they add to your fears? If a fearful mom sets off your own fears, you'll want to be careful about leaning on her in the trenches.

Finding a battle buddy is a great way to remember you aren't alone. When you feel like someone else is "in it" with you, it's easier to remember you have the power to overcome your fears.

5. Trust the one who holds their future in his hands

I think so often about Jochebed and the way she released that basket into the Nile River. It's a picture I can't get out of my mind. She had absolutely no assurance that Moses's life would be spared. Her only hope was in God. So she trusted her son to the one who held his future.

I often catch myself thinking that my way of taking care of my children is better than God's way. Of course that's not something I say out loud, but I think my actions (and my prayers) might say otherwise. When I think like this, I remember Luke 11:13, which reminds me, "If you then, though you are evil, know how to give good gifts to your children, how much more will your Father in heaven give the Holy Spirit to those who ask him!"

We must choose to release our children to God. It's not a one-time occurrence. Very often I say aloud, "God, I release this child to you. I know he is yours, and I know I can trust your love for him." Something about saying the words aloud helps me battle my fear. I also try to remind myself of times when I battled a fear successfully, or times when God showed me he was watching over my child even when I couldn't.

We love our children so much that sometimes we forget we didn't create them. God did. Psalm 139:13–16 says, "For you created my inmost being; you knit me together in my mother's womb. I praise you because I am fearfully and wonderfully made;

your works are wonderful, I know that full well. My frame was not hidden from you when I was made in the secret place, when I was woven together in the depths of the earth. Your eyes saw my unformed body; all the days ordained for me were written in your book before one of them came to be."

We can surrender our children's safety to his sovereignty.

He created them, and before one of their days came to be, he had ordained the whole of their life. God entrusted us with them, and now we need to entrust them to God.

We need not fear what will happen to our children. God has ordained the whole of their lives. All we have to do is love them, guide them, and trust the one who loves them even more than we do.

Action Steps

Name a current parenting fear. Now ask yourself: Is it real or perceived? What is your battle plan for dealing with that fear?

- Who are your battle buddies who encourage you and share their parenting wisdom with you?
- What would it look like to take your fears to God and let go of them, especially when they are fears for things you have no control over?

CHAPTER 6

WHAT IF I CAN'T DO THIS?

Fear of Failure

Writing a book is like walking naked into a crowded room. There's no hiding, no covering up. In the most vulnerable way, you take all your flaws and failures and parade them out in public in front of an audience of strangers (well, and quite a few friends and family, which might actually be worse). It's all there, just hanging out and waiting for the world to see.

This is especially true of *Breaking Busy*, a book that shared how God used my messes and mistakes to show me how to find the confident calm of purposeful living.

As a business coach and consultant, I felt great about writing a book on how to get off the hamster wheel and find confident calm. Great, that is, until I realized that in order to teach the concepts, I was going to have to write about my rough road to learning them. Business concepts, productivity systems? Piece of cake. Writing about my life, about going bankrupt, lying to my girlfriend, trying to bargain with God or avoid him altogether? Was that *really* necessary?

My story and my deepest vulnerabilities would be cast out there to tens of thousands of women. They would essentially know everything about me, and not just the filtered, sanitized, pretty parts of me that I share on Instagram. They would know the ugly parts that don't fit in cute social media posts.

During the writing process I freaked out often when I realized I would have to tell even the most unflattering stories of mistakes and failures if I was going to be real and write a book that could actually help people. But when I turned in the manuscript to the publisher, that's when the worry kicked in to high gear.

What if everyone thinks I'm a terrible person?

What if people read my deepest private thoughts and laugh?

What if no one cares?

And the most painful part was the fear that people would say, "Who does she think she is, thinking she can teach anyone about Jesus? That girl is a hot mess!"

I mean, I might be qualified to teach about business or breaking busy, but qualified to teach about Jesus? No way.

Those worries turned into a full-blown case of fear, more specifically, the fear of failure. During the months before the book came out I spent my free time daydreaming about all the different ways the book could fail.

I spent my time worried that no one would like the book, and that I'd end up like a crazy woman out in the street yelling at people to please buy my book, or showing up at yard sales selling all the extra copies out of the trunk of my car for a quarter each. (I'm not even kidding.)

I worried that release day would arrive and the only sound I would hear would be the crickets in my backyard. Or I worried that people *would* buy the book and would write one-star scathing reviews.

I worried that I wouldn't just be failing my family and my publisher; I would also be failing Jesus.

But if I'm honest, I worried most of all that people *would* read the book and I would be exposed as a fraud, a failure, unworthy of anything and everything. And the fear of that was almost crippling.

I was so focused on what people would think about me that I wasn't focused on the fact that God had called me to write the book. I wanted to be the kind of woman who just focused on Jesus, but I wasn't. Instead I focused on the upcoming exposure of myself to the world and all the ways things could go wrong.

Of course, when the book finally *did* launch to the world, I didn't give a rip about failing. The last thing on my mind was what people thought of me. I was just trying to keep Mark breathing and my family stable.

Nothing like a little perspective sometimes to knock the fear out of us, right?

By the grace of God the book was helpful to women. The message resonated, and many readers used those practical step-by-step tools to change their lives. (There were also some really terrible reviews, and a few times I did hide in the corner, have a pity party, and eat Nutella out of the jar. I'm still wrestling with the truth that you can't please everyone.)

You might think that gaining perspective about my fear of failure allowed me to see how silly it was for me to have been so consumed by it in the first place. But nope, not even close.

Success and even lots of great experience doing something doesn't eliminate the fear of failure. Why? Because fears aren't rational, people, especially the fear of failure!

> Sometimes our successes cause us to come face-to-face with our insecurities.

Even when I felt led to write a book on fear, my fear of failure kicked back in. (Ironic, right?) Tackling a tough topic like fear triggered all my fear-of-failure feelings all over again. I thought, "Who in the world wants to read a book about fear? Writing (or reading) a book about fear sounds about as fun as a root canal."

Over time I have learned that sometimes successes don't translate into security; sometimes they translate into our going deeper into our own insecurities. Because fear is such an effective tool of the enemy, he will keep using it over and over again on us. We have to be prepared for every aspect of fear he throws at us.

A Battle Plan to Fight the Fear of Failure

When the fear of failure comes knocking on my door, I use this little mantra.

> *Show up.*
> *Be real.*
> *Love others.*
> *Don't quit.*

I developed this mantra because when I feel fear getting the best of me, I tend to want to run and hide, put on my mask, bite the heads off of the people I love, and sometimes just flat-out quit.

Let me explain.

1. Show up

Don't let the fear of failure keep you from showing up.

When we struggle with the fear of failure, the idea of hiding at home under the covers can sound really good. (This is classic burying behavior through avoidance. I only teach what I know!) Sometimes half the battle is simply showing up.

One time I got a phone call from the principal at my son's school, asking Mark and me if we could come in for a meeting. I had no idea what he wanted to talk to us about, but of course I assumed I was in some way failing as a parent. What else could he possibly want to talk to us about? It's terrible how our minds go to the worst possible place so quickly.

I can laugh at it now, but at the time, I tried to come up with every possible reason why I couldn't go. I prayed something would come up and I wouldn't be able to go.

On the day of the meeting, as I put on a little lipstick (for Southern women, this is totally part of our battle armor!), I looked in the mirror and gave myself a little pep talk. I said, "Alli Worthington, you are going to put a smile on your face and get yourself in that car. Then you are going to ride with your man and walk right into that principal's office, head held high. You have raised perfectly good children, and you are being silly. There is nothing to fear here. You are going to show up to that meeting. Now get going!"

It might seem silly, but my "show up" pep talks to myself are inspiring in the moment. Positive self-talk for the win! And as it turned out, the principal just wanted to talk to us about being a part of the fundraising team at school the next year. All that worrying for nothing (which is the way it usually turns out)!

2. Be real

Don't let your fear of failure keep you from being who you are.

My defense mechanism when I feel nervous around others has always been to look around, see what everyone else is doing, and make like a chameleon to fit in. If I feel certain I am going to fail as my true self, my logic has always been, why not be someone else, or worse yet, everyone else.

It wasn't until around age thirty-five that I began to wake up to the fact that my fear of failing in social situations was making me disconnect with who I really was and who God had created me to be.

I had to decide to be my real self with others and live out of a place where I liked myself and hoped others would too. Turns out, it was my uniqueness that opened doors for me professionally, allowing me to live out the calling God had for me. God doesn't make us quirky or interesting for no good reason. He gave me, and he gave you, your unique personality to share with the world around you.

As I was talking about the battle plans and fighting our fears, a sweet friend of mine said, "I love it that you talk a lot about fighting and battling, and you are this sweet Southern women who wears bright pink and polka-dots all the time. It's such an amazing combination!" And you know what? It *is* unusual, but it is who God made me, and it's my job to live it out with courage.

We have to fight the temptation to dumb ourselves down, to keep our mouths shut when we know we should speak. Instead, we need to live in the confidence that we are fearfully, wonderfully, and purposefully made just as we are.

To this day, though, when I feel tempted to try to make myself more like someone else to avoid that fear of failure, I tell myself, *Be real, Alli. Be real.*

3. Love others

Don't let the fear of failure cause you to treat others badly.

For me this is a reminder not to let my own fear or worry cause me to be short-tempered with others. My goal is to love others well, even when I'm a mess inside. I don't want fear to control me and turn me into a big ball of nastiness to others.

This is the hardest for me behind closed doors with my family. When I am overly stressed about something with work, or I am afraid a project may fail, I have to work twice as hard at home not to take it out on the family. It's way too easy when I'm staring down a work deadline or even planning a happy celebration to snap at the kids, be demanding to Mark, and make everyone's lives miserable.

Mark and I used to host a church small group in our home every Sunday afternoon. It sounds lovely, right? Multiple families coming over to our house for food, fellowship, and fun, along with Bible study. It sounds like one big Jesus-loving scene. The problem was, and is, I don't have the hospitality gene. I don't. I want to, but Ree, the Pioneer Woman, and me are on opposite ends of the spectrum. She may entertain and feed the masses happily, but I burn the food and want to scream before the masses even arrive. And that's the mindset that ruled our home on Sunday afternoons for almost a year.

The truth is, we all lived in fear of Sunday afternoons. From the moment our feet entered the front door after church, I became momzilla. I amped up my stress and barked out orders to the kids for hours. "Jack, take the giant pile of clothes off the couch and hide them in one of the upstairs bedrooms." (Y'all know you have a giant pile of clean laundry somewhere in your house just waiting to be folded!) And, "Joey and James, get all of the shoes and sports equipment and shove it under my bed. Just don't let me forget where it all is later." I didn't want to "fail at small group," so I became the cleaning tyrant for four hours every Sunday. It was pure misery.

Instead of being focused on us all having a good time, I focused on "winning small group hosting." I wanted it to be the best time *ever.* I was so not going to fail at small group. No way.

By the time our guests arrived each Sunday afternoon, I was exhausted and tense, the kids were shell-shocked and annoyed, and Mark had just given up.

Welcome, friends!

(Not so much.)

I wasn't focused on loving others; I was focused on performing well and not failing. It took me some time, a long time, but I eventually woke up to the fact that no one cared if my baseboards were clean, but they all felt the low-grade tension lingering in my house when they arrived. I was treating my family terribly and making others feel uncomfortable, all out of a place of fear.

When I'm tempted to treat others badly, I repeat my battle-plan mantra: "Show up, be real, love others, don't quit."

4. Don't quit

Don't let the fear of failure, or anything else for that matter, cause you to quit (hello, bowling class). We can only truly fail when we quit trying.

I find the temptation to quit occurs most often when I am in the middle of a project or job, fearing I will fail, and I decide that quitting (and being labeled a quitter) is so much better than failing (and being labeled a failure).

Like I said, fear is not rational and does not cause us to think clearly.

Have you ever said to yourself:

- I didn't know it was going to be this hard.
- I can't do this anymore.
- I'm not good enough.
- What was I thinking when I thought I could do this?

You are in pretty good company. The secret is to strengthen yourself not to quit.

Sometimes, even after I speak my mantra, I struggle to overcome the fear of failure. When that happens, I take Scriptures and personalize them with my name, like this:

- "I, Alli, have been brought to fullness in Christ, who is over every principality and power" (from Colossians 2:10).
- "I, Alli, have the peace of God, which transcends all understanding, and it will guard my heart and my mind in Christ Jesus" (from Philippians 4:7).
- "I, Alli, am God's handiwork, created in Christ Jesus to do good things, which God prepared in advance for me to do" (Ephesians 2:10).

I call these passages my "Don't Quit" verses. When I remind myself of the things I can do *in God's strength*, the voice of the enemy gets quieter and quieter until I can't hear the lies anymore.

When we remember to show up, be real, love others, and not quit, we don't have to control anyone else or the outcome of what we do. We get to bring our best to any situation with courage and love.

The results are up to God; he just asks us to be who he called us to be, love others, and do our best.

Not All Failure Is Equal

Recently I was watching my cousin's adorable toddler as she put together a puzzle. She must have failed thirty times before she finally got that puzzle finished. But those little failures didn't cripple her. She didn't stop after a few tries and declare, "I have failed at puzzles and will therefore forever be a failure at all things."

She learned from each failure and kept going.

As adults, we don't typically develop the fear of failure from all failures either, because all failure is not equal.

For example, have you ever tried out a new recipe when friends were coming over for dinner, only to have the new recipe be a complete flop? Did that keep you from ever cooking again? Probably not.

Have you ever tried to play a game you've never played before and failed miserably at it? Probably so, but I'll bet that didn't keep you from showing up at family game night, did it?

Have you ever wondered why that is? Why some failures we brush off and some break our hearts?

The reason some failures don't instill a fear of failure in us is because the result of that failure doesn't impact our life for the worse; there's no emotional weight to the failure. If I fail at a new recipe, my life is not going to be terrible. If I lose at Dutch Blitz, I'm not going to be labeled a failure in the world's eyes. I'm not emotionally invested in those things.

But let my business go belly up (or my book be a horrific embarrassment), and that adversely affects my family's financial security. Let me not get it right as a mom, and that affects my kids' future. Let me be a failure as a wife, and that affects the future of my marriage.

Our own fear of failure isn't the fear of failing in and of itself; it's that we fear what the results of that failure might be: rejection, loss, financial destruction, and loneliness.

But what if . . .

What if even in the big things we could believe that failure is the rich soil where our faith grows?

What if we believed failure was full of new insights, wisdom, and self-knowledge?

Failure is the rich soil in which our faith grows. What if we could see that failure filled us with humility, gratitude, and even a little grit from the battle?

And most importantly, what if we believed God doesn't see our failures, but sees our future and holds it all in his hands?

I can't help but think if we looked at our failure through the eyes of God, we wouldn't fear it in the least. God sees every one of our missteps as a new opportunity to trust him. I like to imagine him saying, "You failed marvelously today, Alli. Your faith is growing!"

Breakfast with Jesus

If anyone knew about failure, it was my favorite disciple, Peter. He wanted to do right, but he was always doing wrong. That's a man after my own heart right there. I believe God appreciates those of us that are do-ers, even if we make a bunch of mistakes along the way. At least we are trying. Peter is such a great example of a do-er!

Imagine the scene in John 21. The disciples followed Jesus for three years, thinking that he was going to establish his kingdom on earth any day now and that they would be ruling with him. Then they saw him crucified. Just weeks before they were arguing over who would be most important in a new earthly kingdom, and now they were alone, scared, and devastated

And I can't help but think that Peter would have been the most devastated of all. He had rejected Jesus.

He failed Jesus in the worst way.

But God was not finished with Peter (nor was Peter finished with failing).

After Jesus was crucified, Peter and the other disciples didn't know what to do, so they returned to what they knew: fishing.

One night, they fished till dawn, but didn't catch a thing. In the morning, a man on the shore called to them, "Children, do you have any fish?" As we know from Scripture, that man was Jesus, and you know that he knew full well they didn't have any fish.

Jesus told them to cast their nets on the right side of the boat, and they obeyed, and then watched in amazement as their nets filled with fish.

John recognized Jesus. Then Peter, ever the impulsive one, leapt into the cold early morning water of the Sea of Galilee. But he didn't walk on water this time. In his excitement, he swam the whole way to the shore!

When Peter arrived at the shore, he found Jesus cooking up some breakfast. Jesus wasn't angry with him, didn't lecture him on his various recent failings, or remind him of his gift for being impulsive and messing things up. No. Jesus came and offered love, understanding, and a hot breakfast.

Peter could have stayed on that boat, stuck knee-deep in the pain of his failure. He could have allowed that pain to separate him from God, but he chose the outstretched hand of Jesus.

I don't know what that reunion must have been like on the beach that morning, but my heart can imagine it. Peter released the pain of his failure and accepted the healing that Jesus had to offer.

The pain of our failures has to be released to God so we can be restored.

Likewise, the pain of failure has to be released to God so we can be restored and reconnected.

My friend, what kind of pain of failure have you felt? Have you ever been devastated and gone back to what you knew? What does that look like in your life?

We know from this story in John that Jesus isn't waiting on the shore of your heart to blame or condemn you. He's there to love you, to encourage you, and maybe even to cook up some breakfast.

Getting Past Our Past Pain

We hold onto the pain of past failures until they become woven into our hearts and minds. But that is not what Jesus has for us. In order to heal from the pain of our past failures and overcome the fear of future failures, we must practice our ABCs: acknowledge our feelings, ban the B's, and choose to believe Jesus.

1. Acknowledge our feelings

Maybe it's a lost business, a failed marriage, a friendship that ended over an argument—whatever it is, it's important to acknowledge the feelings you have about the failure.

Remember, the enemy doesn't want us in touch with our emotions, because you can't heal from what you don't feel.

2. Ban the B's

When we are battling the fear of failure, it is so easy to fall back on these coping mechanisms.

- We *busy* ourselves trying to make sure our perfect kids stay that way. (Because, after all, any sort of failure from one of our kids is a direct reflection on our ability to mother them correctly, right?)
- We *binge* eat our way through a package of Double Stuf Oreos rather than face certain failure in another relationship. (It won't work out. It never does.)
- We *blame* anyone and everyone for why we failed the last time and let that be the reason we don't risk failure again. (If those ladies weren't so dumb they could have seen that I was the best choice for the PTA.)
- We *bury* our feelings altogether because out of sight, out of mind. (I never really wanted that job anyway. Whatever.)
- We *brood*, constantly replaying our failure until it becomes a deeply rooted fear. (What was I thinking? Why did I say that? If I had only made a different choice that day.)

If you want to be free from the fear of failure and the pain of the past, you have to ban the Bad B's.

3. Choose to believe Jesus

Brennan Manning, in his book *Ruthless Trust*, completely changed how I viewed my own failings in light of the gospel: "Wallowing in shame, remorse, self-hatred, and guilt over real or imagined failings in our past lives betrays a distrust in the love of God. It shows that we have not accepted the acceptance of Jesus Christ and thus have rejected the total sufficiency of his redeeming work. Preoccupation with our past sins, present weaknesses, and character defects gets our emotions churning in self-destructive ways, closes us within the mighty citadel of self, and preempts the presence of a compassionate God."[1]

Isn't that said so beautifully? When we truly accept the total redeeming work of Jesus, we have no choice but to decide we are going to stop beating ourselves up.

Because we will all fail. This is a reality of living on this planet. We all fail and will continue to fail. What matters is how we respond to our failure. We can choose to believe that Jesus can rewrite our stories and use our failure for his good (and ours), or we can become stuck in a cycle of failure.

A perfect example of this is the woman at the well.

The woman at the well was a mess. She was a failure in the eyes of her community. She was stuck in a cycle of failure, failing over and over again, marrying one man and then another and then another and then another and then another, until she gave up on marriage entirely and just lived with a guy. Her fear of failure eventually became the assumption of failure until it became actual failure.

The woman at the well feared that her life was colored by such failure that she could never rise above it.

But then Jesus showed her differently.

He knew her stories and her pain and offered her life and a future.

He addressed her failed relationships, but what he really wanted to do was show her that she had a bigger purpose in the kingdom despite her failure. And she believed him. So she left her water jar behind, went back to her town, and said to the people, "Come, see a man who told me everything I ever did. Could this be the Messiah?" (John 4:29). And what happened next? Did they blow her off? Did they say, "What do *you* know? You're not even married!" No. They all came out to meet Jesus.

Jesus broke the cycle of failure by speaking truth to her. Just like he is breaking the cycle by speaking truth to us today.

"Yes, you had five husbands and are living with someone outside of marriage. So what? It doesn't have to be your story. How would you like to lead people to eternal life?"

In the same way, he speaks truth over you and me today.

- "Yes, you got fired from that job. So what? It doesn't have to be your story."
- "Yes, your marriage fell apart. So what? It doesn't have to be your story."
- "Yes, your child rebelled. So what? It doesn't have to be your story."

You can choose to believe the truth that Jesus has a purpose for you beyond your failure and allow him to rewrite your story.

Our futures are already claimed by God; we don't have to stay stuck in a cycle of fear and failure.

Failure doesn't have to be your story. He is still writing your story.

Embracing Failure's Hidden Gifts

From our children's perspective, just imagine how many things they mess up every day. From the toddler and the puzzle, to learning to ride a bike, to long division, to learning to drive a car. This process of growth is just a long string of failures until success is reached. In our adult lives, we still have long strings of failures until we master things too! Anyone who has watched a YouTube video and decided they can install their own toilet can attest to this. Good things take time and lots of mistakes as we learn along the way. But in our success-focused, achievement-focused culture, failure is right up there with death. No one wants any part of it, but have you ever considered that there may be gifts hidden in our failures?

Failures mean you are doing something. The enemy of our souls wants us stuck, fearful, insecure, and powerless. He wants us to be so afraid of failure, of ridicule, of any potential loss, that we sit on our hands on the sidelines of life and grow old.

God, on the other hand, isn't shocked by your failures, your mistakes, or even your biggest screw-ups. He's not in heaven saying, "Hey, Jesus, look at how Alli is messing up lately. I had great plans for her life, but this month alone she managed to forget to pay her car payment, gossiped about a friend (when she knew better. I know the Holy Spirit tried to warn her when she got on the phone that day), and decided to stay home and watch a football game in her PJs instead of go to church. I guess that ends those great plans we had for her."

Of course not. That's crazy talk. But isn't that what the devil wants us to believe? He waves our failures in front of our faces, trying to convince us that we have no value to God. What a liar.

The lies of the enemy will tear you down, but the truth of God's grace will build you up. No one is ever motivated to do better by criticism and shaming. But that's what we often do to ourselves, isn't it?

Constantly going over our mistakes doesn't motivate us to do a better job in the future and make sure we don't mess up again. Instead, it actually makes everything worse! Focusing on our mistakes leaves us feeling more anxious and upset!

When I'm tempted to beat myself up over some failure, I've learned that instead of being self-critical, repenting and showing compassion to myself is healthier. For example, I might tell myself, *Yes, it is super disappointing that I forgot to send out the car payment. I do have a lot on my plate, and I will make a note on my calendar so it doesn't happen again. Yes, I shouldn't have gossiped. I'm sorry, Lord. Help me keep my mouth in check. And about that football game? Lord, I needed that rest, and the football game was great, but help me just DVR the game so I can make it to church to worship next week.*

We all make mistakes; the key is to learn from them, and (as Elsa sings) let them go. Brooding doesn't make things better. But admitting our mistakes, repenting of them, and asking God's help to do better (then trusting him to provide that help!) will help us make those much-needed changes.

I believe one of the most important things we do as parents is live out failure well in front of our children. When we struggle and fail, we pick ourselves up, dust ourselves off, and keep going. Trying and failing and trying again is one of the best things we can model for our kids.

Practice self-compassion, not self-criticism.

If we are living and breathing, we are going to fail, mess up, and make mistakes, over and over again. How we respond to our challenges, failures, and mistakes will shape the way our kids face challenges in their lives. You set your kids up to be successful in life by modeling how to handle failure.

When kids grow up afraid of failure, and don't have a concept of how to handle failure when it comes (and you know it will!), then they are more likely to grow up scared, passive, and unable to live out the calling God has given them.

When we live our lives accepting that failure is a normal part of life, we can live with the confidence that when we fail, God will strengthen us and show us the path for recovery, allowing us to fulfill whom he has created us to be.

Battle Plan Against the Fear of Future Failure

We all have the tendency to assume we will fail again because we have failed in the past. Of course this is an assumption at first, but the longer we believe that is true, the more likely it is to become true. We can overcome the fear of failure if we take action. Baby steps, my friend, baby steps!

1. Give yourself grace

Jesus continually shows compassion for his followers, even wild Peter who had so many of his own failures. Jesus shows love, kindness, and grace. If Jesus looks at us with grace and love, who are we to continually beat ourselves up?

Practice self-compassion, not self-criticism. In other words, give yourself some grace.

2. Give yourself time

We all have the tendency to want a magic list of steps or activities that will make things better and ease the pain of a failure. It's okay to take the time to feel the sting of the failure. Don't bury those feelings, but don't brood over them either. Remember the old adage, "This too shall pass." It may not pass as soon as you want, but knowing the pain of failures (big and small) takes time to heal will help you be kinder to yourself in the process.

3. Give yourself permission

Give yourself permission to accept the failure and learn from it. Identify what you can change about how you will handle a similar situation in the future. Just like the toddler who learned from her failures while putting her puzzle together, if we choose to learn from our failure rather than wallow in it, we can overcome the fear of future failure.

The enemy is set on convincing us to believe that we will eventually fail in such a big way, Jesus will have no choice but to reject us. When we learn to see ourselves through the eyes of Jesus, to acknowledge our failures as a normal part of life, and to allow him to write the end of all our stories, the fear of failure will have no power over us.

Action Steps

Check out page 211 for the "Don't Quit" personalized Bible verses to speak over your life.

- What failure have you struggled with recently? Is it a failure in your past, or a fear of failing in the future?
- How does Jesus see that situation? Ask him what he wants you to learn from it.
- How can you practice self-compassion instead of self-criticism?

CHAPTER 7

WHAT IF I GET HURT AGAIN?

Fear of Betrayal

Before becoming my business consulting client, Melissa had a career as an executive in a medium-sized, privately-owned company. She loved her job, she was successful at it, and after fifteen years, her coworkers felt like family. Melissa had just received a promotion and a big raise before leaving for a family vacation, where she focused more on the sand between her toes than on the spreadsheets waiting for her when she returned.

After her vacation, she received a text message from her boss, asking her to meet early Monday morning before the office opened. In all the years in her job, the only time anyone was ever asked to come in early was when someone on the team was getting fired. She told her husband, "Man, what a way to end vacation. I have to go in early tomorrow. I guess someone is getting fired."

In that meeting, Melissa discovered *she* was the one being let go. Her boss explained that in her absence some situations had come to light, which led them to believe they couldn't trust her anymore. Her termination was immediate.

Shell-shocked, Melissa sat dumbfounded for a few minutes. When she was able to speak again, she asked for details of these alleged situations. He gave her three. Each example had elements of truth, but the versions her boss relayed were either greatly exaggerated or twisted into stories that weren't even close to the truth. The one common denominator in all three stories was Melissa's coworker and best friend, Karen.

Melissa pleaded her innocence. She asked, "Does this even sound like me?" Her boss said no, but offered no other information. She suggested getting everyone in the room to talk about it, face to face. Surely fifteen years should have earned her that opportunity, right? But no matter what she suggested, her boss just said, "No. I'm sorry. We've made our decision."

On the drive home from the meeting, Melissa realized she had not only lost her job, but the community she had come to love, as well as her best friend.

Sensing that her friend, Karen, might be behind the allegations, Melissa began to replay different moments with her friend from the past few months. She knew something had seemed off. Repeatedly she'd asked Karen, "Hey, are we okay? Is anything wrong?" But Karen always reassured her, saying, "No, we're great. I've just been so busy." Perhaps she should have pressed harder. Her head throbbed and her heart hurt over the realization that something had gone way wrong in their relationship, and she had been blind to it.

At home that day she tried to call Karen, but there was no answer.

She texted her. No response.

She tried to send her a Facebook message, and that's when she discovered she had not only been unfriended, she had been blocked.

Her mind reeled.

What could have possibly happened between them that was so terrible, and how in the world could she have been oblivious to it?

She slowly woke up to the realization that while she was on vacation, for reasons she didn't know, her best friend in the world set her up to be fired.

As she told me the story, she paused to say, "I know what this sounds like. Trust me. I know it sounds made up. That's been the hardest part, knowing this doesn't make sense to anyone. And if it doesn't make sense, then I must be making it up, right?"

She found herself stuck in the stinging pain of betrayal combined with the added pain of rejection by her employer and coworkers. Not only that, but in the small town where she lived, her sudden termination became the talk of the town.

She was a well-trusted leader in her community, active at church, in civic organizations, and at school. In the eyes of others, Melissa must have done something heinous to be terminated immediately. The very next Sunday at lunch after church, one of her friends had the audacity to ask her if the company was going to press charges. Melissa said, "What? Why would the company press charges?" Her friend said, "Well, for you to just get fired out of the blue, we thought you might have mismanaged money or something."

Over time, she felt more and more cut off from her friends and fellow coworkers. It seemed to her that everyone either "knew" what really happened and just wasn't telling her, or everyone assumed the worst about her, despite years of a life to the contrary.

The combined pain of betrayal, rejection, and abandonment caused such deep pain that Melissa closed herself off and left the house less and less. She found herself brooding, continually questioning why this happened to her.

She was angry at her former friend, at the boss who wouldn't listen to her (or to the truth), and at God for letting this happen. Her anger soon turned to resentment, then bitterness, then hopelessness. And she sank into a very deep depression, at times even considering suicide.

Melissa's fear of future betrayal stopped her from seeking out new employment. The thought of putting her livelihood into the hands of someone who could just as easily toss her aside was too scary. She was frozen in fear.

But Melissa didn't have the luxury of not working. Her income was crucial to her family. So on the advice of a friend, she took her talents and started an online business. (This is how we met! I had the honor of walking with her through the process step by step.)

In her isolation, she spent a lot of time questioning everyone and everything. The enemy worked overtime to convince her that if she couldn't trust her best friend and people she had known for years, then surely she couldn't trust God either.

But in the midst of that pain, crying out for truth, she remembered the one place she could always find it: in Scripture.

She held tightly to verses like these:

> The LORD is close to the brokenhearted
> and saves those who are crushed in spirit.
> The righteous person may have many troubles,
> but the LORD delivers him from them all;
> he protects all his bones,
> not one of them will be broken. (Psalm 34:18–20)

As Melissa found truth in Scripture, she began to realize the lies of the enemy. Today, after many years of healing, Melissa runs a thriving business of her own, and she has learned she can trust others and have healthy friendships. The Lord redeemed the situation for his glory.

Melissa said, "The same pain that I thought was breaking me, was making me into who I am today. I learned that even though I might not ever have all the details or the answers or understand the why, I could trust God. He knows the truth, and that is enough."

She never learned the real reason her best friend betrayed her in that way. And even though they are both still living in the same small town, they haven't spoken in five years. That's the way life is. Sometimes the story doesn't end with a pretty bow tied around it, you know? But that doesn't change the fact that even though we might experience betrayal and rejection at the hands of broken people in a broken world, we can still trust God for our good.

Betrayal might break you, but God won't forsake you.

David, a Man After God's Own Heart

Remember David, the shepherd boy who was anointed by the prophet Samuel to one day be king; who slayed the giant, Goliath, with a single stone; and who served King Saul with humility, then became king himself?

This was a man who knew all about betrayal.

> The king he served became obsessed with him and wanted to kill him (1 Samuel 19).
> David's son Absalom revolted against him to try to steal his throne (2 Samuel 14:25).
> One of his closest advisors, friends, and confidants, Ahithophel, betrayed him and conspired with Absalom (2 Samuel 15:30–31).

Over and over, throughout his life, David experienced betrayal at the hands of those he loved. But when Ahithophel betrayed him by taking sides with his son, who was also betraying him, he couldn't take it anymore.

David's first response was to allow himself to experience the pain of betrayal. He did not minimize his sense of hurt. He poured it out to God. David shows us that we, also, need to acknowledge when we have been hurt, and instead of turning our pain inward, turn it over to God.

David writes,

> If an enemy were insulting me,
>> I could endure it;
> if a foe were rising against me,
>> I could hide.
> But it is you, a man like myself,
>> my companion, my close friend,
> with whom I once enjoyed sweet fellowship
>> at the house of God,
> as we walked about
>> among the worshipers. (Psalm 55:12–14)

Next, David realized he needed to change his behavior. He recognized that he could not trust his friend in the same way. He goes on to say,

> My companion attacks his friends;
>> he violates his covenant.
> His talk is smooth as butter,
>> yet war is in his heart;
> his words are more soothing than oil,
>> yet they are drawn swords. (Psalm 55:20–21)

And then watch what David does. In the midst of his pain and betrayal, he reminds himself of the truth he knows about God (and he doesn't mince words, either).

> Cast your cares on the LORD
>> and he will sustain you;

he will never let
 the righteous be shaken.
But you, God, will bring down the wicked
 into the pit of decay;
the bloodthirsty and deceitful
 will not live out half their days.
But as for me, I trust in you. (Psalm 55:22–23)

David responded to the pain of betrayal by going to God and laying it all out to him. He didn't pretend like he wasn't hurting. He allowed himself to feel the grief and the pain, and he poured it out to God.

I can just picture him shaking his fists in the air, saying, "But you, God, will bring down the wicked into the pit of decay; the bloodthirsty and deceitful will not live out half their days."

I've never personally called anyone bloodthirsty during a prayer (yet), but I have definitely used some choice words to describe people. I have learned from David that God wants us to cast our cares upon him . . . and by cast, he means "let it all out."

Intentional Versus Unintentional Betrayal

Just as David experienced betrayal at the hands of someone he loved, and just as Melissa experienced betrayal at the hands of someone she trusted, you too may have experienced intentional, premeditated betrayal at the hands of someone close to you. Intentional betrayal happens when someone *willfully* decides to hurt you for some reason, be it selfishness, personal gain, or because they are just flat-out terrible.

There is, however, what I like to call an "unintentional betrayal." As I prepared to write this chapter, I realized I may very well have committed who knows how many acts of accidental betrayal in my life.

I've been guilty of not keeping a confidence because I didn't realize the seriousness of the information.

I've not shown up to a gathering that I promised I would attend. (I'm a high functioning introvert, and sometimes I just need to stay home.)

I've chosen to spend time with one friend, at the expense of time spent with another friend.

Does this make me a horrible person? I hope not.

Does it make me an occasional flake? Maybe.

Friend, all of us make mistakes. Sometimes, despite our best intentions, we inadvertently hurt someone we love dearly, or are hurt by someone who never meant to hurt us.

Yet the accidental, unintentional, all-too-human betrayals can hurt just as much as the vicious, calculating, premeditated kind.

Why?

Maybe it's because they make the world seem unsafe, or your relationships precarious. Or maybe it's because it reminds you of your own failings. Or maybe it's even because you sense a darker presence at work, something that lurks, waiting to destroy your most precious relationships (see 1 Peter 5:8).

Betrayal, whether premeditated and intentional or accidental and unintentional, is real, and none of us are immune to it, which is why we have to know how to respond when we have been betrayed.

What to Do When You Have Been Betrayed

1. Make sure you haven't misconstrued the situation or been overly sensitive

Sometimes, what feels like an intentional betrayal to us could actually be an oversight or mistake or human error on the other's part (see above), or it could be a gray area.

For example, imagine two college friends, Amy and Kristin.

They both are interested in the same guy, John. The guy really is fair game. But Amy declares her interest in John first and assumes she has "first dibs" and everyone else should back away. But then John asks out Kristin, who accepts because she too is genuinely interested in John. Amy may *feel* betrayed by Kristin, but no actual betrayal has occurred. John is free to choose a date, and Kristin is free to accept.

I had a betrayal gray area circumstance in my own life. When Mark and I got married, we had to pay for it ourselves. My family wasn't able to help out because they simply lacked the financial means. This meant we had a very small, intimate wedding with just our family and a few close friends. A year after our wedding, I heard through the grapevine that an old high school friend was livid with me, but I had no idea why.

Only when I called her and asked her point blank if she was upset with me did she tell me it was because she hadn't been invited to my wedding. I apologized profusely and explained that my budget only allowed for a few friends. Just imagine the hurt my friend felt all those months! She had told herself a false story about the situation, turning it into an intentional personal slight against her.

Sadly, there are many people who choose to be overly sensitive about the smallest of offenses. I recently had to pull back from a friend because after years of being emotionally drained every time I talked to her, I just couldn't take the drama anymore. Whenever we talked she told stories of people who had slighted her, offended her, or in some way, shape, or form mistreated her. In my opinion, 99 percent of the time her stories of betrayal were without merit. These people were just living their lives and never meant to hurt her. But my friend carried deep unhealed wounds that resulted in a strong spirit of offense, so strong that every situation gave her a new reason to be upset.

At least three times a week she would call and tell me all the details of the latest drama, and I would try to talk her through it and help her realize she was making the choice to be offended. Unfortunately, my well-intentioned efforts just offended her more! The friendship was at an impasse, and I dreaded seeing her number pop up on my phone. I started to ignore her calls and send them to voicemail. And if I returned her calls, I made it clear I wanted to talk about things other than people who had annoyed us recently. Over time, she started calling me less and less, and now instead of three times a week, she calls me three times a year. I still love her, but I can only take her in small doses.

When you see the world as a victim, you will react as a victim, and seeing every interaction through the lens of a hurt heart can allow the enemy to lie to you and tell you that you should be offended. But it doesn't have to stay that way. If you, while reading this section, felt a nudge that you may have a tendency to react from a hurt heart, please remember you don't have stay stuck. Ask Jesus to heal the deep hurts of your heart.

2. Accept what happened and allow yourself to grieve

Betrayal often triggers an avalanche of painful emotions. For many of us, when we sense that avalanche of pain coming our way, we bury those emotions, pretending we are magically "over it" and acting like we have healed in miraculous time. We bury the pain before it can bury us.

We have to feel our pain to heal our pain. But if we want to heal from the pain of a betrayal, we must allow ourselves to experience not just the betrayal, but also the emotions that come with it. We have all heard the experts say that if we don't allow ourselves to feel the pain, we can't heal from the pain. (Don't miss this just because it seems cliché.)

Melissa's experience of her friend's betrayal was real, and it felt like the unexpected death of a loved one. The betrayal resulted in the sudden and final ending to her job and to her relationship with someone very close to her. She described the feeling as a deep sense of grief.

Grief is an acceptance that something you once had is now gone. We grieve lost relationships, lost jobs, lost health, and loss of security. And the more you love something, the greater the loss feels, and the deeper you grieve.

Melissa had to learn to allow herself to grieve *all* of her losses, not just of her job and her friendships, but she also needed to grieve the loss of her ability to trust. Through the grieving process she learned how to admit the hurt of her betrayal and eventually learned to forgive.

Until you can admit the hurt you feel from a betrayal and talk about it with someone safe who has earned your trust, you can't fully heal (or fully forgive), because you will never allow yourself to be open and vulnerable again.

Admitting the hurt that your heart is already feeling allows your heart to finally feel heard and validated.

3. Be responsible with your pain

Accepting betrayal and the pain that goes with it is a necessary step on the road to healing. But we need to be responsible with the pain of those emotions and not allow ourselves to be controlled by them, destroying other relationships in the process.

Four months after her initial betrayal, Melissa was caught in a pattern of brooding over what happened and why it happened, replaying every situation over and over in her mind. She wasn't eating well or sleeping well, and she lived in a constant state of anger and resentment. Melissa's personality changed too, and she went from confident and secure to suspicious and controlling.

One rainy night her husband came home late from a meeting, delayed because of the storm and the terrible traffic. When he walked in the door, she lost it. That night her husband told her in the most loving way he could that she had been short-tempered and super suspicious with him and their children ever since she had lost her job. It was only after that conversation with her husband that she decided to try counseling through her church.

When we can sense our emotions are out of control, we have to allow ourselves to feel the pain, but we must also be responsible with our emotions. This might mean leaving the room, asking for time to process something before responding, going to counseling (like Melissa did), or going on a personal retreat so that the intensity of your emotions doesn't wash over innocent bystanders and damage other important relationships.

4. Confront your betrayer (or seek to understand the betrayal)

One of my friends discovered her husband was having an emotional affair with a coworker. He had left his Facebook account open on their shared computer, and she saw a series of messages between her husband and the woman at his office.

> Out-of-control emotions do not have to become out-of-control behavior.

In the course of just a few days she went from shock, anger, and hurt, to blaming herself. She blamed herself for not being the perfect wife, not having sex enough, not being thin enough, and not being happy enough for him, and she set out to win him back instead of confronting him on his betrayal. She never told him she knew.

Her focus was on convincing her husband she was a worthy wife and not on the fact that he had betrayed her trust.

Over time, her behavior became controlling, and he emotionally pulled further and further away. Because of her fear, she never spoke to him about his stepping over the line. Her pain, turned inward on herself, destroyed her. Unfortunately his emotional affair and the unhealthy cycle of the relationship ended in their divorce.

Could the marriage have been saved if she confronted him with what she knew? I don't know, but I do know that denial and turning pain on ourselves never ends in healing.

We can't work our way out of our pain. We have to be honest and let ourselves heal.

When we have been betrayed, it is healthy to confront the person who betrayed you. Acting as if it didn't happen out of fear of further loss only makes the situation worse.

Whether it is your spouse who has overstepped emotional boundaries with a friend, or a coworker who stole your idea and took credit for it, bring these things into the light and don't automatically blame yourself or believe the lie of the enemy that you deserved it.

In Melissa's case, she didn't have the chance to confront her friend because her friend would not talk to her. So in order to grow toward forgiving her friend, she had to seek to understand the betrayal.

She didn't blame herself for her friend's betrayal, but as she prayed for understanding, she began to see that somewhere along the way she must have hurt her friend (albeit unintentionally) in such a way that it caused her friend to lash out. She realized that her friend probably had a deep wound and that somehow she had flipped the trigger switch attached to her friend's pain. As she began to imagine her friend's pain, she started to release her own pain and had genuine sympathy for her friend.

5. Begin the ongoing process of forgiveness

I'm a big fan of forgiveness, when I'm the recipient of that forgiveness, of course. But when I'm the one that needs to do the forgiving, I tend to find forgiveness overrated.

When I hurt someone I'm all about mercy and grace, but when I get hurt I am tempted to ask God to rain down hellfire.

Obviously I'm kidding (sort of), but my point is that forgiving isn't easy.

And yet, we must forgive much because we are commanded to "be kind to one another, forgiving one another, just as in Christ, God forgave you" (Ephesians 4:32).

But sometimes we don't want to forgive because forgiving almost seems like we're letting the person who hurt us off the hook.

Forgiveness doesn't mean that the betrayal is okay. It doesn't mean what the person did to you is okay. Forgiveness is a gift to yourself, not a release of guilt to the offender. It sets you free from the weight of carrying around all that hurt and anger.

When we carry around hurt and anger, it festers and grows into a spirit of bitterness and offense. When our hearts become bitter and offended we live life wounded and see every interaction through the lens of that pain. When we have offended and bitter spirits, we aren't free to live life in the way we are created to live.

There is great power in forgiveness.

Melissa's own healing began when she decided to forgive her friend. For months she carried around the weight of her painful emotions, longing for a face-to-face with her friend so she could let her have it. But as time led to healing, and as those hurtful emotions began to subside (as they often do), she started to realize the pain her friend must have been in as well, pain that caused her to lash out in betrayal.

Melissa knew she needed to forgive Karen, not for Karen's sake, but for her own. And so she prayed, *God, will you forgive me for the things I must have done to hurt my friend Karen? And like-wise, I forgive her for the pain she has caused me. When I remember her, let me remember her with love and fondness for all the great years of friendship we had together.*

Once Melissa truly forgave her friend Karen, she said she began to feel truly free from the bitterness of betrayal and from the fear of future betrayals the enemy had tortured her with for months.

6. Decide on the future of the relationship

Your friend may have hurt you unintentionally and be genuinely remorseful (or blissfully ignorant). In that case, you may decide to let bygones be bygones and continue the relationship, only with certain new boundaries in place. In other cases, your friend's intention was so clearly malicious, or the offense so serious (such as adultery), that tough decisions must be made. In these cases, I advise seeking out wise counsel from a counselor, pastor, or seasoned mentor.

Just talking through the situation with someone else will help you clarify the issues, process the emotions, and perhaps even arrive at a next step toward healing. Pray too for the Spirit's guidance in this process, trusting that he can bring good out of what the devil meant for our destruction (Genesis 50:20).

7. Be extra good to yourself

When we get hurt we may feel numb initially, or lash out in anger, but often we turn our pain inward on ourselves. It is one of the enemy's oldest tricks. If he can't convince us to doubt and reject others, then he convinces us that we are somehow unworthy of the love of others.

Self-blame and self-loathing are common reactions when we've been betrayed. A key is to be extra good to yourself, practicing self-compassion and not self-criticism.

When you find yourself reeling from a painful situation, it's a perfect time to practice self-care. It's critical that you get plenty of sleep, make good food choices (even though that carton of

FIERCE FAITH

Ben and Jerry's calls my name when I'm upset), and stay active. Sitting around typing and then deleting passive-aggressive social media updates is not a healthy choice (not that I know anything about that, of course). But when you focus on feeling better, you will be protected from feeling bitter.

When I am hurting, I spend extra time telling Jesus about everyone that hurt me, going for walks, listening to worship music, snuggling my man, and planning a movie date with a girl-friend. We are each wired differently and find comfort in different ways. Whatever works for you is best, as long as it moves you toward healing and not just further down the road of bitterness.

Focusing on feeling better protects us from feeling bitter.

It is true that past painful experiences can set us up to fear future painful experiences. But betrayal, rejection, and heartbreak don't have to leave open wounds that affect us forever. There are ways that you can protect yourself from the fear of betrayal.

A Battle Plan to Fight the Fear of Betrayal

You will be scared of being hurt again. That's normal. But don't stay stuck.

1. Understand that one painful experience doesn't have to color your whole future

Every summer I look forward to the return of our backyard hummingbirds. To lure them in, we have five different feeders, some attached to our windows, some hung from trees, and some on hangers in the far corners of our backyard. And as they zoom around at a million miles an hour, all day long, they bring our family so much happiness.

Every Sunday afternoon, I make the hummingbird food

solution of water, sugar, and a few drops of red dye. My little guys love to watch the final step of making hummingbird food when we drop those ten drops of red food coloring into the water. A whole pitcher of water is transformed by a few little drops of red food coloring. With one quick stir the water turns red.

Isn't that what a painful experience does to us? The sting of betrayal, the pain of rejection, and the grief of abandonment can color our lives just like those few drops of red dye.

The only way to get the red dye out of the water is to keep pouring fresh water in until it runs the red out. When we are hurt we have to keep pouring in what is good, what is healthy, and what is helpful until the pain of betrayal is run out.

If we aren't careful, betrayal can cause us to have trust issues for a lifetime, causing us to close ourselves off and not risk being hurt again.

For example, Melissa developed unreasonable expectations of what people should do and how they should behave. In counseling she became aware of her hair-trigger response to anyone even remotely questioning her integrity. So over a period of about eighteen months, she prayerfully and intentionally worked to relearn how to be a good friend and how to have grace for her other friends all over again.

Melissa is a great example of someone who learned to leave the past in the past. And her future has brightened as she has become confident and trusting once again.

2. Be mindful of when your "trust triggers" are flipped

Just like the light switches on our walls, sometimes certain situations trigger us and we can flip on or off in an instant. When we get triggered, it becomes more difficult to trust the love, good intentions, and even the loyalty of those around us. Here are some common situations that trigger us not to trust:

- When you have plans with someone and that person cancels at the last minute.
- When you see your friend post pictures of the party that you weren't invited to.
- When a coworker takes credit for a project you worked on together.
- When your husband's attractive coworker comments on his post on Facebook.

One of the things I learned from Melissa is to say, "This is just triggering my rejection switch. I know

When our trust triggers get flipped, we flip out

that person isn't betraying or rejecting me. I am just taking it that way."

Being mindful of my own trust triggers and saying Melissa's phrase above is so helpful.

3. Know that you can always trust Jesus

When we put our trust in Jesus, we know we are putting our faith in the one person who will never disappoint us, never hurt us, never betray or abandon us. As Jesus reassured us, "I am with you always until the very end of the age" (Matthew 28:20). And God tells us: "Be strong and courageous. Do not be afraid or terrified because of them, for the Lord your God goes with you; he will never leave you or forsake you" (Deuteronomy 31:6).

Memorizing Scripture that reminds us of Jesus's faithfulness and presence in our lives is a great tool in battling the enemy.

Betrayal is one of the most painful things we can endure because most often it comes at the hands of those we care the most about. Betrayal can temporarily steal our security and leave us with wounds that feel like they are killing us.

We do not have to live in fear of the future, but can trust that in him our future is secure. If you have been living life carrying the pain of betrayal, and living life feeling unloved and unlovable, I want to remind you that you can begin to heal today. You can overcome the pain of betrayal with God's help and live in the security of knowing he is with you and will never betray you.

The enemy's lies cannot withstand the power of God's truth.

Action Steps

Ask God to open your eyes and give you courage to revisit a time you felt betrayed. Was that betrayal unintentional or intentional?

- Have you been able to forgive the person who hurt you? If not, ask Jesus to help you begin the process of forgiveness.
- What are some of your trust triggers? What happens when they get flipped?
- What are some things you can do to be good to yourself when you are feeling betrayed, rejected, or abandoned?

CHAPTER 8

WHAT IF EVERYONE HAS FUN WITHOUT ME?

Fear of Missing Out

You might be thinking, *What on earth is a chapter on FOMO doing in the midst of serious discussions of fear of betrayal and loss?* We have been diving into some pretty heavy topics that bring up a lot of heartache. I wanted to lighten things up a little.

And without being overly dramatic, we have to talk about this whole fear of missing out thing. It's such a big deal that it has its own acronym! FOMO gets to us on such a deep level that we can't just ignore it (especially in a book about fear). FOMO is familiar and pervasive and real. I think there's real power in naming it, claiming it (cringing at it), and doing battle with it.

Recently, some of my girlfriends decided to go on an amazing girls' getaway weekend to Las Vegas. The plan was we would all leave Thursday evening and be home by Sunday night. Three days away visiting spas, going to fabulous restaurants, and seeing big, wonderful shows.

I was happy to be included, happy to listen to all the details of the plan, but in the end, I decided not to go. I'm in a very full season of life. Mark and I have five boys, and you can imagine all the activities (and time needed) that go along with the boys.

I also travel between one and three times a month for work and speaking engagements. I really didn't want to leave my family again, even though I knew the trip would be fun!

By the time you read these words in book form, my oldest will be a freshman in college (pray for me. Oh, my heart!). And our "baby" will be in third grade. In ten years, I'll have all the time I want to travel and get away with friends, but for now, in this season, Mark and I both are dedicated to spending as much time with the boys as we can.

So I happily declined the chance to go to Vegas and cheered my friends on as the weekend grew closer. I had a great weekend planned anyway: I was taking the boys to see *Finding Dory*, and Mark was cooking out for us on Saturday. It wasn't a gourmet meal in a five-star restaurant, nor was it Cirque du Soleil (though in my house something equivalent could break out at any time), but I didn't need those things. I was happy.

And then Friday happened.

Friday, midday, I started seeing the pictures go by my newsfeed. All three of my girlfriends who went on the trip were having the time of their lives. Beautiful meals were getting Instagrammed, the incredible spa was being Facebooked, smiling happy faces of my girlfriends having a blast kept getting posted, Tweeted, and snap-chatted, and I was bitter and, honestly, a little mad at them for going without me.

FOMO hit me like a ton of bricks.

I was missing out on all the fun, and even worse, I was watching the fun happen in real time.

My lovely weekend with my family, that I was so happy about before, no longer measured up.

By Saturday morning, I had managed to start a fight with Mark, snap at two of my sons for no good reason, and eaten my body weight in waffles, PBJs, and carrot cake with cream cheese frosting. I was a mess. And I blame Vegas.

Here's the thing. I don't even like Vegas.

The first time I ever went to Las Vegas, I landed in the airport and was greeted in the restroom by an elderly woman in a tube top and a miniskirt. Rearranging the money she'd stuffed in her tube top, she smiled at me and said, "Welcome to Vegas!"

I'm a small-town girl at heart, so the flashing neon, the sound of slot machines constantly dinging, the tube tops and stilettos, and the overall "feel" of Vegas just isn't my thing. So turning down the girls' weekend to a destination that I didn't like and that I didn't want to leave my family for was an easy decision.

But it sure did seem like the wrong decision with every photo my friends posted.

Celine Dion singing "My Heart Will Go On" while wearing a fabulous sequined dress and dancing in high heels? Ugh. I missed it.

Cirque du Soleil's grand performance with people doing impossible stunts while wearing the coolest costumes ever? Ugh. I missed it.

By Saturday night I had had it. But I couldn't stop looking at the photos. The happier my friends got, the more unhappy I got.

Every picture I saw on social media made me jealous and sad I didn't go. I wanted to be in those pictures, not at home cleaning vomit out of the rug (you don't even want to hear that part of the story).

The more fun they had, the more my own life seemed bland, bad, and boring.

I was missing out on all the fun, all the future inside jokes, all the memories with the friends that I love, and I wasn't going to be in those pictures. I wanted to be in the pictures! I wanted to be having fun! I did not want to be scrubbing the rug and cleaning up after our family cookout.

By Sunday afternoon after church (which really *should* be the time when I'm thinking clearly after all that time worshiping Jesus, I know!), I took a turn for the worse.

Here are some examples of where my thoughts were:

- They are all having fun without me.
- What in the world am I going to post on Instagram if I'm not with everyone else having fun?
- My life is so boring.
- I never get to do anything fun.
- What can I post that makes me look like I'm having more fun than they are?
- What if they talk about me while I'm not there? What would they say?
- Am I overreacting? No, I'm most definitely not!

Not my finest moment.

But that's how it is when we're in the middle of a FOMO attack.

FOMO is normally associated with missing a life experience. But it also encompasses the fear of feeling left out and like we don't belong.

But FOMO as a term has taken on a whole life of its own. It is not only used for being afraid we are going to miss out, it's also a social media phrase we use to express when we feel left out, and to justify doing things just because everyone else is doing them.

FOMO: When We Feel Left Out

I'm a girl who loves events, conferences, and gatherings. I love them. I love to host them, attend them, speak at them—I love it all. There's something about people coming together to learn, to focus in and hear what God is saying, to share their wisdom, and to build community that gets me every time.

Giant arenas with thousands? I want to be there.

Auditorium of hundreds? I want to be there.

Room of ten? Sign me up!

Small, invite-only gatherings are very popular these days. Weekends at a spa, a ranch, or in another country with a select group of people are constantly getting posted on Instagram.

I'm embarrassed to say that photos of these experiences flip all my rejection switches. There have been at least ten times in the past few years I've been going along in my day, having a good ol' time, and something I see flips those switches, and all of a sudden I feel rejected and left out.

I will see a group shot on Instagram of a group of my friends doing something awesome that I wasn't invited to. I should just think, *Man, they look they are having fun!* But instead I simmer and stew in a deep pot of envy.

The more mature Alli is actually happy for them. She knows she doesn't need to be invited to everything. Everyone should be happy and free to post pictures of all their great times. It is not a slight against anyone else.

But the forever thirteen-year-old Alli is hurt. She wishes they weren't bragging about how awesome life is while the highlight of her day is unplugging the toilet. She broods, blames, and buries like a boss.

FOMO: When We Go Along with the Crowd

My FOMO has caused me to make some terrible decisions (and that's just as an adult. My adolescent years could be a case study in it!). FOMO has caused me to chase Pokémon around my neighborhood, almost start a podcast because all the cool kids were doing it, go vegan (for a day), and dye my hair pink. The list could go on and on.

I'm currently battling the whole *life-changing magic of tidying up* phenomenon. It seems like everyone I know is posting pictures of themselves tossing their belongings and finding a new level of joy in their minimalist environments. Apparently you are supposed to throw away everything that doesn't bring you joy.

I imagine myself throwing away my bathroom scale, the elliptical machine, the broom, and all my bras.

But still, I'm tempted to buy the book everyone is raving about and start purging away.

When I asked my girlfriends on Facebook what they have done in the middle of a FOMO attack, I got some great answers. Here they are in the classic Jeff Foxworthy format of "You might be a redneck if . . ."

You might have FOMO if . . .

- you take pictures of other people's fancy meals to post on your own Instagram account.
- you dress your kids up in nice clothes and pose them for your "casual" family shots just for Facebook.
- you spend your whole day scrolling on Facebook to see what everyone else is doing.
- you feel jealous when looking at updates from other people.
- you see pictures of family members at a social function that you would rather pull your toenails out than go to, but you're hurt that you weren't invited to attend.
- you buy a gift with money you don't have to go to a party or shower for someone either you don't know or don't like, to be around the people who are causing your FOMO.
- you've pretended to be outdoorsy just to go on a camping trip with friends. And been eaten alive by mosquitoes and cried yourself to sleep in your sweaty sleeping bag.

Again, this is a judgment-free zone. I've done many of these myself. But if you nodded and giggled seeing yourself in these examples, it's important to be aware of FOMO and have a battle plan to protect yourself from the pain caused by future attacks.

Because we live in a time where we have a world of information, images, and videos coming at us constantly, FOMO isn't going to go away. In a world of constant connection, FOMO, and its evil twin, social comparison, are the struggles of our time.

Because of social media we are able to see the most fun, most amazing, most exciting handpicked moments in hundreds of acquaintances' lives, all in real time. And if you've just cleaned up a diaper blow-out, gotten fired, or are hanging around eating Cheetos on the couch when you see those posts, FOMO pops up and whispers to you just how terrible your life is.

FOMO also makes us afraid of regretting something. Regretting that we missed a chance at something, regretting that we didn't say yes to an opportunity, and regretting that we feel alone, less than, like a failure.

Here's what we know about what FOMO does to us:

- FOMO causes us to use social media more often. In other words, the more FOMO you have, the more you will be on social media.[1]
- Fifty percent of teenagers feel they are "missing out" on the seemingly perfect lives that others show on social media.[2] (I'd bet this number is similar in adults.)

But FOMO existed long before social media and iPhones. It's been around pretty much since the beginning of time.

Biblical FOMO

I know Eve gets a lot of blame for causing the original sin and all, but let's take a minute to think about the underlying reasons. Could one of them be FOMO?

There she was, just minding her own business, all the while listening to Adam naming every last thing in the garden, having himself a ball, swinging from vines and yelling, "Eve, you have *got* to do this!" Suddenly, from out of nowhere, up slithers that evil serpent, convincing her she is missing out on something big, something God doesn't want her to have.

Suddenly, maybe, she felt discontent.

The enemy wields the weapon of discontent through FOMO and it spreads like a virus. Listen to how he convinced Eve that she only "thought" she had it all. Watch how he created FOMO in her, despite her truly perfect life.

> Now the serpent was craftier than any of the wild animals the Lord God had made. He said to the woman, "Did God really say, 'You must not eat from any tree in the garden'?"
>
> The woman said to the serpent, "We may eat fruit from the trees in the garden, but God did say, 'You must not eat fruit from the tree that is in the middle of the garden, and you must not touch it, or you will die.'"
>
> "You will not certainly die," the serpent said to the woman. "For God knows that when you eat from it your eyes will be opened, and you will be like God, knowing good and evil."
>
> When the woman saw that the fruit of the tree was good for food and pleasing to the eye, and also desirable for gaining wisdom, she took some and ate it. She also gave some to her husband, who was with her, and he ate it. (Genesis 3:1–6)

See what the enemy did there? He planted the seed of longing in her, a seed of discontent that made Eve certain she was missing out. The enemy robbed Eve of the joy of her present circumstances and convinced her to trade that in for a chance at what she was missing.

Just let that sink in for a moment. Isn't that exactly what I did when I saw my friends in Vegas? Because of FOMO I traded in the joy of my present circumstances just to envy their joy.

And if that weren't bad enough, Eve had to bring Adam into her FOMO state of mind. Adam was doing stuff in the garden, wrestling bears, skipping rocks, and, well, I don't know, other man stuff. He had no idea he was missing out on anything until Eve made him aware of his own FOMO.

I can just imagine the scene in the Garden of Eden.

"Adam, I have the most exciting news. The *best* thing just happened. You have got to try it!"

Adam probably resisted for a moment, but then I imagine he too was captured by the fear of missing out, and he caved in to the call of FOMO.

Later in the Bible, we read the story of the prodigal son and his equally epic case of FOMO. There are not many details given us in Scripture as to *why* he asked his father for his inheritance, but I like to imagine FOMO had a part in it. He must have felt the world outside his homeland offered something he was missing, and he had to have it at all costs.

Just like Adam and Eve, he had everything: a stable home, a loving father, everything he could possibly want or need there at his fingertips. And just like Adam and Eve, he gave up everything to answer the call of FOMO.

And that's the way FOMO is. It's highly contagious. We've been catching it from each other ever since. The problem now is we catch it in real time from millions of people!

What happened to Adam and Eve and to the prodigal son is the same thing that happens to many of us. We question, "If we stay here, in this place God has created for us, within the confines and safety of his will, will we be missing out?"

Some ways this plays out include:

- A teen who chooses to skip a gathering of friends, but then sees the crazy fun pictures and feels like she may have missed out and then posts, #fomo #nexttime, on her social media account.
- New mothers who question their decision to quit work and stay at home with their baby—or their decision to find childcare and return to work. This can be the most serious case of FOMO ever!
- Young parents who feel called by God to place their kids in public school (or home school, or Christian school), but worry when their choice is different than what their friends or church community is doing.
- A mom who blows the family budget to keep up with the Joneses, whether that is in housing choice, vacations, or children's clothing and extracurricular activities. (I know a thing or two about that one. Ahem.)

Knowing that the enemy uses FOMO to draw us outside of the circle of God's will is the primary reason we must have a battle plan to fight him.

A Battle Plan to Fight the Fear of Missing Out

When I was in the middle of my Vegas-induced FOMO attack, I called my friend Megan. After she listened to me complain, feel sorry for myself, and blame my friends for going without me, she asked one simple question:

"Do you really want to be in Las Vegas, the city you hate, instead of where you are right now?"

Hmm.

The phone went silent.

"Not really," I whispered, like a kid caught stealing a bite of cake left out on the table.

"Alli, c'mon. Let's be realistic here, your friends did not leave you behind. You chose not to go. Maybe you secretly wanted them to cancel the trip because you couldn't go. Maybe you wanted them to say, 'Well, without Alli, there is no party. No reason to go now!'"

By this point in the call, I was just grunting indecipherably on my end of the phone. Megan doesn't pull any punches, that's for sure.

"And seriously, Alli, get off social media. Do not post anything on Instagram. That is super passive-aggressive. Your friends, whom you told to go, whom you cheered as they planned their trip, are not posting things to hurt you. But right now you're taking everything personally. Nobody's paying any attention out there in social media world that you aren't with your friends. You need to redirect your energy to something that's not about getting shallow outward validation on Instagram and Facebook. Turn off your phone, go be with the family you adore, and do what you actually love to do."

I don't even remember what I said back to Megan after that. It was mostly grunts and some form of "Alright I guess you're right. Whatever." But I knew she was right. I had a decision to make. I was either going to get my head on straight or I was going to stay stuck, feeling sorry for myself and dissatisfied with my life.

I learned a lot about myself and how to battle FOMO from my lost Vegas weekend and my "real talk" with Megan. Like everything else in my life, my pain (or lesson) is your gain!

Next time you feel an attack of FOMO coming on, try these steps.

1. Check yourself

The first step is to check yourself (in my case, it was to have Megan help me check myself). When you are feeling left out or like you're missing out on something amazing, ask yourself some version of the following questions:

- Do I really want to be there instead of here?
- Is that what's really important right now?
- Am I feeling jealous of someone else's fun or success?
- Is that really my lane to run in? How can I stay focused ahead in my own lane?
- What do I want that I don't have right now?
- Do I have PMS? (Seriously, I always get FOMO when I'm hormonal.)

Most of the time if we go through the process of asking ourselves the tough questions, even when we are upset and emotional, the answers bring freedom.

2. Name the underlying emotions

Some have argued that FOMO is a combination of anxiety and envy. (Ouch, that kind of hurts, doesn't it? No one likes to think of themselves as being envious.)

But when we think about all the different ways in our lives that we feel FOMO, one or both of those two emotions tends to be a root cause.

As I watched my sweet girlfriends have the time of their lives, I felt both anxiety and envy.

My anxiety caused me to question my own sense of security. Was I okay? Was I enough? Was my life good enough? Do my friends really still love me?

And in my envy I wished I were doing all the things they were doing in that moment. I wanted to go spend a lot of money in the spa, eat fancy dinners, and go see all those shows. But I have five kids, a mortgage, tuition, and lots of sets of braces.

Recognizing our ugly emotions like anxiety and envy, then naming them and claiming them (even when they're uncomfortable), actually helps us move past the very short-lived fear of missing out.

3. Switch your FOMO into JOMO

"Turn off your phone, go be with the family you adore, and do what you actually love to do."

I had become so focused on what my friends were doing I was neglecting my family at home. Instead of enjoying what was right in front of me, the people I loved most in the world, I was wasting my time, ruining my own happiness.

And Megan was right to call me out on it and tell me not to post anything on Instagram. We can't try to stage joy for shallow validation from people out in social media land; instead, we have to find joy with the people who share our homes and hold our hearts.

The way not to buy into the fear of missing out is by opening our eyes to what surrounds us right now, finding the magic in our lives, because often it's hidden in plain sight.

When we see what is wonderful around us we can change our FOMO into JOMO: the Joy of Missing Out.

4. Do happy now

Gratitude changes FOMO to JOMO.

This is one of my favorites. *Do happy now* means going for the quick win. Do something you love immediately: go for a walk, snuggle your kids (or your nieces and nephews), watch your favorite movie on Netflix, love on your pets, read a good book, or do whatever it is you do that always puts a smile on your face.

Just a word of caution on this one, though. Don't give in to negative ways of alleviating your FOMO, strategies like retail therapy (no matter how great you'll look in those shoes) or overindulging in your favorite foods or certain beverages. Those things might make you happy in the moment, but down the road, they will be much worse for you than the worst case of FOMO.

The great news about FOMO is it is temporary. When you are

in the middle of a FOMO attack, going for the quick win, the fun distraction, or even a quick cuddle from someone you love will usually be enough to let those FOMO storm clouds pass on by.

5. Reframe your thoughts

There is a very cool technique that therapists use called reframing. Essentially it means we take our thoughts or situations and look at them with a new lens, or put them in new frame.

When we feel sad, we frame all situations negatively. Our thoughts are more negative. When we feel angry, we frame things in an angry way. The secret is taking a step back and looking at our thoughts and reactions to see if we can reframe them.

After my call with Megan, I realized all the negative thoughts were playing in a loop and making everything look bad. I happened to have a hair elastic around my wrist, so I decided that for the rest of the weekend, every time I found myself brooding, blaming, or doing any of the five Bad B's, I'd snap that hair elastic. It wasn't hard enough to hurt, but it did serve as a silly reminder.

Reframing your thoughts allows you to regain your peace.

It was so silly, so simple, and amazingly it did make me aware of how often the negative thoughts were dragging me down. Just being aware helped me remember to let out a little "help me, Jesus" prayer, take my thoughts captive, reframe them, and direct my energy back to my family.

Reframing thoughts is a cool trick for battling FOMO. For example, instead of thinking of my friends in Vegas having fun without me and feeling sorry for myself with thoughts like this:

Must be nice to go to Vegas and have all that fun. I'll just be here cleaning the rug.

I reframed it to:

I chose not to go to Vegas because when I'm there, I don't like it there.

I'm home with the family I love.

Here's an example of reframing when it comes to social media, where we compare our real life to everyone else's hand-picked amazing moments.

It's easy to look at the achievement of someone else on the Internet and minimize our own progress. When you feel that happen, take a step back, and look at how far you've come, everything that you've learned, how hard you've worked, and be glad that there are trail blazers a few steps ahead of you in the journey that you can look to and learn from.

Instead of saying,

She is so successful; she must just have a natural gift. I don't have what she has. I'll never be as good as her.

You can reframe it like this:

I love what she has done. I can learn from her successes and wisdom as I work to reach my dreams.

Or maybe you're envious of someone's stage of life or station in life. They're married; you're not. They have a baby; you don't. They have a cool career; you're home with the kids or slogging away at a dead-end job or struggling with a debilitating illness. Instead of saying,

I wish I had a life like hers.

You can reframe it like this:

I am fearfully and wonderfully made by a loving heavenly Father. God has a plan for my life, and I'm excited to see what he has in store for me. I know his plans for me are for good and not for evil, to give me a future and a hope.

Name those unhealthy all-too-human thoughts. Then reframe them using God's Word. You'd be surprised at how powerful this simple tool can be.

6. Stay focused on Jesus

Five years ago, I wouldn't have included this section on staying focused on Jesus to battle FOMO. I would've found it too trite, too easy, too Sunday school lesson-ish. But as I've grown, and walked with Jesus a little longer, I see now that if I'm focused on him, he helps me squash the feelings of envy with gratefulness, his acceptance replaces my feelings of rejection, and his presence fills up my loneliness.

It is only by keeping focused on him and trusting his plans for me that I can silence and defeat the work of the enemy and his tool: FOMO.

God will make sure you are exactly where you are meant to be.

Jesus said, "Do not let your hearts be troubled. You believe in God; believe also in me" (John 14:1). His command is so clear, so simple—"Do not worry, believe in God, and believe in me."

He makes our paths straight; he guides us along still waters; he restores our soul; he knew us before we were born; he sees our lives from beginning to end; and he alone determines our destiny.

He's teaching me that if I'm meant to do something, or I'm meant to have something, or if I'm meant to be included in something, I will be. Where he wants me is where I'll be.

Because I know he holds the future, I don't have to fear that I am missing out. On *anything*.

Action Steps

Go to page 213 for a space to practice reframing your thoughts.

- Think of a time when you felt FOMO because you were afraid you would miss out on something. What happened?

- Is there a certain situation that always flips your FOMO triggers? How can you prepare for these situations?
- What strategy will you use to battle the enemy next time you have a FOMO attack?

CHAPTER 9

WHAT IF THINGS FALL APART?

Fear of the Future

Erin, an incredibly talented designer and married mother of two girls, hired me to help her launch her own graphic design business. Erin loved the idea of starting her own business. She craved the control that being the boss would give her; she wouldn't have to move her husband and daughters to a new town for a new job, and she could be home for her daughters after school.

She wrote, "Alli, I've had the dream to start my own business for so long, and now seems like the perfect time to take the leap. I just need help getting where I want to go."

And for Erin, the "perfect time" to launch was thrust upon her when she learned her company was downsizing and her position as creative director was being eliminated immediately.

The good news for Erin was she had the capital to get started, courtesy of a killer severance package, and she had a built-in main client, her old employer (*which is the best safety net ever for starting a new business*). The bad news, I found out quickly, was Erin was secretly paralyzed by the fear that her business would fall apart. One day, during a coaching call with me, she listed out all the things that could go wrong:

What if there was a terrible economic downturn?

What if she had a health crisis?

What if all the design jobs got farmed out to Asia?

At this point in my life, I can spot fear of the future a mile away. I've been through it myself. Back in 2007, when my husband's job was eliminated, we found ourselves over-mortgaged, in way too much debt, unwilling to move our family away from Tennessee, and within a year, bankrupt and homeless. (If you've read *Breaking Busy* you know all of these details, and I won't bore you again. If you haven't read it, I hope you do!) I know all too well the overwhelming fear that everything is going to fall apart, because for me in many ways it did. And like Erin, I too had the perfect time to start a business thrust upon me, so I understood her deep-seated fear that she didn't have what it takes to build a business. Been there, done that. That's why I spend so much of my time helping other women start and build businesses!

I explained to Erin that yes, starting a business for the first time can seem overwhelming, but we have enormous resources at our fingertips. Thanks to the Internet we can learn anything we need to learn, we can start our own businesses at very little cost, and we can plant our proverbial stake in the ground and build what we dream of without needing anyone's permission. We have at our fingertips a world of information and resources. What an amazing time to be alive!

Over the next six months Erin and I worked together, step-by-step, on the foundations of her business, how to package her services and products, the back-end systems that would keep it running smoothly, her branding position, and her marketing plan. Everything was set up behind the scenes, and Erin was finalizing touches on her website, preparing for her public launch.

Then the phone call came.

That one phone call changed everything.

Erin called me and told me about her conversation with a recruiter looking for a creative director for a startup in Houston.

It's a great job. Should I take it? I mean, I don't want to move us to Houston, but it's a paycheck. A solid, stable paycheck. I won't have to worry so much about the future. I won't have to worry about my cash flow drying up because of an economic downturn."

On the Cusp

Erin was on the cusp of launching her own business, fulfilling a dream she had had for over fifteen years. The website was built, the financial invoicing system was prepared, the LLC was filed, her clients were lined up . . . but one thing wasn't ready.

Erin.

Erin knew she could do the job. She knew she was great at design. She wasn't afraid of failing. Erin had a fear of the unknown future. Her fear of the future, the future she couldn't control, ended up being greater than her desire to run her own business.

The week before the planned launch of her new business she put everything on hold and prepared to fly to Houston for an interview. From the airport on the way home she called me to discuss their offer.

It was a great offer, her husband was willing to relocate, and to her, the security of full-time employment looked too appealing in the moment to pass up. So she took the job.

Could she have opened the business and been very successful? Of course she could. She had the talent, she had clients, she had all the resources and help she could need. Her future was bright and filled with hope. But she couldn't see it because she couldn't face her fear of the unknown future.

Our future is filled with hope. But if we are going to face our future, we must face our fears.

No matter how great the business plan was (and it was great, if I do say so myself), no matter how many clients were lined up to fill her days with meaningful work, no matter how many systems were developed to keep the business flowing smoothly—the fear of the unknown future, the nagging suspicion that things would fall apart, and the hopelessness that followed, were too much for her to bear.

Erin put her business idea on the shelf, put their belongings on a moving truck, and let the fear of the future steal her dream.

And just like Erin didn't recognize that her fear of the future was what was holding her back, we often don't realize our own fear of the future is stopping us in our tracks, keeping us stuck, and wondering why we have a low-grade suspicion that we aren't really living the life we were created to live.

Your dream for the future might not be career related. It might be a desire to adopt a child, a calling to lead a small group, a yearning to finish your degree, a desire to take those ballroom dancing lessons you always dreamed of, or a wish to start a farmer's market in your town.

The enemy of our souls wants to distract us, delay us, and discourage us with fear.

The enemy of our souls has always used the fear of the unknown to keep us stuck. Instead of forging forward into the Promised Land, we wander around, lost and lonely in our own wilderness.

Just ask the Israelites. They should know. After all, they were the wizards of wandering.

Stuck in the Wilderness

The Israelites had been slaves in Egypt, but finally, freed from bondage, led by Moses, they were headed to the Promised Land! The journey across the desert was a long one, but over that time, God proved his faithfulness to his people again and again. When they feared that the Egyptians would slaughter them, he drowned the armed forces that pursued them. When they feared getting lost in the vast tracts of the desert, God sent a pillar of cloud to guide them by day and a pillar of fire to guide them by night. When they were hungry, he fed them with manna and quail. And when they were thirsty, he sent them water out of a rock.

Finally, after their long journey, they were on the verge of reaching their destination. As they sat outside the Promised Land, God said to Moses, "Send some men to explore the land of Canaan, which I am giving to the Israelites" (Numbers 13:1).

Just stop for a moment and reread those words. Notice the Lord says, "Explore the land of Canaan, which I am giving to the Israelites." He didn't say, "If it looks good, I'm going to give it to y'all," or "If things don't seem too crazy over there, I'm going to give Canaan to the Israelites." No, God was quite clear about his intentions. "Take a look around," he was saying, "because everything you see is going to be yours one day."

So Moses chose the twelve leaders, one from each tribe of Israel, and sent them out exploring. And when they returned, at first they gave a glowing report. *Yes, the land is flowing with milk and honey! Wow, look at these grapes, they're huge!* But then ten of the spies turned pessimistic. Instead of focusing on God, they looked at themselves, and this is what they concluded: "We can't attack those people; they are stronger than we are. . . . The land we explored devours those living in it. All the people we saw there are of great size. . . . We seemed like grasshoppers in [comparison]" (Numbers 13:31–33).

Just look at how quickly the Israelites lost sight of who they were—God's people—and how he'd saved them! Instead of keeping their focus on God and his promises, they started comparing themselves to those around them, cutting themselves down, and even calling themselves "grasshoppers." Even with the assurance of God and having witnessed his power to save them, ten of the twelve spies were so overcome by insecurity and fear of the future they were willing to wander around in the wilderness, waiting for a better plan.

Isn't that the way fear of the future keeps us stuck in the wilderness ourselves? We are so busy looking for the perfect set of circumstances to line up with what we think we must have, we completely miss out on what God had for us all along.

It doesn't have to be that way. Sure, we are afraid. Joshua and Caleb were afraid too, but they didn't let their fear of the unknown keep them from claiming the Promised Land. (And just think, only Joshua and Caleb's names were recorded in the Bible! All the scared guys? Their names are scrubbed from history.)

But despite the plea of Joshua and Caleb to take the land God had promised them, the Israelites chose to walk in their fear instead of into their future. As a result, the entire nation of Israel was made to wander in the wilderness for forty years. Of the men of their generation, only Joshua and Caleb were allowed to enter the Promised Land at the end of that forty-year exile.

Stones of Remembrance

After Moses died, God appointed Joshua as the leader of his people. And finally, at last, God gave the signal that it was time for the Israelites to cross the Jordan River and enter the Promised Land. He told Joshua,

> "Be strong and very courageous. Be careful to obey all the law my servant Moses gave you; do not turn from it to the right or to the left, that you may be successful wherever you go. Keep this Book of the Law always on your lips; meditate on it day and night, so that you may be careful to do everything written in it. Then you will be prosperous and successful.

Have I not commanded you? Be strong and courageous. Do not be afraid; do not be discouraged, for the Lord your God will be with you wherever you go." (Joshua 1:7–9)

So we see here Joshua has a *mission*. He is to lead the Hebrews to the Promised Land out of the wilderness where they have been wandering for forty years. (Forty long years. Can you even imagine?)

We see that Joshua has God's *promise*. God promised that the land was his, that no one would be able to stand against him, that he was the leader to lead them out, and that the Lord would be with him.

We also see Joshua has *instruction*. He is to be strong and courageous, to be careful to obey the laws Moses gave him, to study the book of instruction, to not be afraid or discouraged.

Those were some marching orders!

As Joshua was leading the Hebrews, God dried up the Jordan River to allow the Ark of the Covenant and the entire nation of Israel to pass by. It was a miracle! To commemorate this miracle, God told Joshua to have a man from each tribe pick up a large stone to build a memorial. Joshua then told the Israelites, "In the future when your descendants ask their parents, 'What do these stones mean?' tell them, 'Israel crossed the Jordan on dry ground.' For the LORD your God dried up the Jordan before you until you had crossed over. The LORD your God did to the Jordan what he had done to the Red Sea when he dried it up before us until we had crossed over. He did this so that all the peoples of the earth might know that the hand of the LORD is powerful and so that you might always fear the LORD your God" (Joshua 4:21–24).

Yes, the Israelites were afraid. Afraid to enter the Promised Land. Afraid to fight the battles that awaited them there. But by picking up stones and building a reminder of God's faithfulness, they redirected their fear.

Focusing on God's faithfulness frees us from fear.

When I was younger, I didn't notice this story about building a memorial of God's work, but as I get older, and face more and more uncertainty about the future—whether it be with my family, with geopolitical unrest, or with financial markets—my eyes are wide open to the power of those stones of remembrance, memories of times when God intervened in my life.

My own stones of remembrance include:

- After the loss of a son from miscarriage, God graciously gave us another son.
- God blessed me by supplying clients and contracts when I first started my business.
- After I prayed for a mentor in the faith to encourage and teach me, God sent a wonderful woman to me.

When we stand at the edge of our own next step, our own uncertain futures, the enemy will always try to stop us with fear. He has been doing it since the beginning of time, and he knows all our weaknesses and insecurities. The enemy of our souls fights hardest when God is doing a great work in our lives.

But we know that he who has overcome the world lives in us. We know that victory is his, and even though we face a battle today, the enemy will not be victorious. We fight from a place of victory because of Jesus. We don't have to fight *for* victory, because it is ours already!

Taking the time to remember God's faithfulness redirects our fear and urges us forward to claim our next Promised Land.

Giants in the Land

Of course God didn't hand Canaan over on a silver platter. Instead, he asked his people to invest some sweat equity: knock down some walls, clear out the underbrush, and drive out the squatters. By rights, the land was theirs—God had told them so—but they had to stake a claim.

And that claim brought them toe-to-toe with giants, strong warriors that had to be defeated in battle, seemingly impassible city walls that had to be torn down, crafty enemies that needed to be outwitted.

You may have set one tentative foot into your Promised Land only to face what looks like an undefeatable giant. God never said that claiming your Promised Land would be easy. But he did say, "Be strong and courageous" and "I will be with you" and "Obey me, believe, and be faithful."

When Mark and I lost everything and God told us he would rebuild our lives, believing didn't come easy. When God told Mark he wanted him to stay at home and raise the kids while I supported the family, obeying didn't come easy (for either of us). And when God told me multiple times to switch gears (close BlissDom and build a consulting company, then put everything on hold to help build Propel Women), being faithful didn't come easy. The giants of doubt in those situations were forever in the forefront of our minds.

The enemy sends out his giants when we are living in our calling and on our way to our Promised Land. He hits us in the places we value most: our faith, our family, and our finances. This is absolutely what he did with Mark and me.

But what if we started looking at these attacks, these dark seasons, as normal passages of pain from the wilderness to the Promised Land of our calling, of our future? And in that frame of mind, where we are reminding ourselves that our dark seasons are part of the journey, what if we reminded ourselves that the enemy is 100 percent invested in keeping us in the wilderness while God is 100 percent invested in guiding us to the Promised Land? Wouldn't that give us hope as we face our giants?

He tells us so in Isaiah 41:10 where he says, "So do not fear, for I am with you; do not be dismayed, for I am your God. I will strengthen you and help you; I will uphold you with my righteous right hand."

I've learned God's presence doesn't mean I'm fearless; instead, it means I can fear less. But that lesson was learned only after a long, hard battle.

In the week before Christine's call to me encouraging me to fight, in the midst of my darkest days, crying in parking lots, scared for my family and Mark's health, I went to Jesus and prayed over and over, and in my heart I heard the exact same reply again and again.

God's presence doesn't mean you are fearless; it means you can fear less.

I am with you.

I wish I could tell you those words were comforting at that time, but those words filtered through my fear and pain just made me angry.

I would say back to Jesus,

Don't tell me you're with me when I feel like everything is falling apart.
Don't tell me you're with me when you can heal Mark right now but you don't.
Don't tell me you're with me when I am on my face begging you to move mountains.
I don't feel like you are with me, and I'm scared.

I had believed the lie that God's presence wasn't enough. And I had begun to tell myself the story that everything was hopeless and things were not going to change. All I wanted was to go back in time, back before it seemed like my life was falling apart.

Don't Look Back

The lie of fear tells us that the future holds pain, loss, and failure. But the past is no refuge either.

Remember Lot's wife? She knew what the past held in her sordid little hometown of Sodom, but she was so unsure of the future, she couldn't help but look back as her past life went up in flames. Talk about stuck in the past—God turned her into a pillar of salt for trying to hold on to something he'd already destroyed.

The Israelites too learned that hanging onto the past led to dreadful consequences, if only same ol', same ol'.

Same ol' manna.

Same ol' quail.

Same ol' dreary desert landscape, swirling sand, temporary tents, wandering around in a state of boredom and discouragement and purposeless apathy.

Sometimes life kicks us out of the nest. We lose a job. An accident or illness waylays us. Someone we love dearly passes away. And as much as we might want to crawl back into that old nest (prickly as it might be), we can't. Our past has gone up in flames, and our future is staring us in the face.

Will we retreat to our own desert and squat there, moaning and groaning and walking in circles? Or will we get up and take our first steps into the Promised Land?

In that painful season of hopelessness, I lay in bed at night and dreamed of ways to get my past life back. Back to the days when the enemy wasn't worried about me and wasn't attacking, back before Mark got so sick, back before life seemed so hard and the future seemed so hopeless.

Whenever we are doing kingdom work, we will be attacked. Kingdom work is anything that's done in love for the greater good. It doesn't necessarily mean you're working in a ministry.

Your kingdom work may be teaching your children, loving your husband, caring for an elderly parent, serving those in need, or just doing your job so you can provide for your family.

Everyone doing kingdom work needs to strengthen themselves for battle.

Whatever your kingdom work is, it is holy, it is important, and the enemy will take notice. And it doesn't have to be bad things that sweep away all our security and everything we know and love. The challenges of young married life might make us long to be single again. Having a baby might make us wish for the freedom we had pre-Pampers. When our children grow to be wonderful young adults and leave the nest, we might feel lost and depressed walking the same halls that used to be filled with little feet. Friends, you can't look back. You can't look back and at the same time expect to walk confidently into your future.

When we are battling the fear of the future, we are stuck between where we have been and where we're meant to be. It's the messy middle, the in-between, the doldrums, the valley. It's always hard in the in-between. It's simply part of the process. You can't run back to the past. There are only two options: stay stuck forever or battle on.

I'm telling you that you can do it. You can fight, and you will get through this. Don't stay stuck in that messy middle; keep walking to your future.

When we spend our lives life looking backward, we rob ourselves of the future God has planned for us. When we are walking out of the wilderness and facing a fight, it feels terrible and the safety of the past comes calling.

God wants to strengthen us to face the future. He is building each of us to be the person he created us to be. And sometimes, to reach our promised future, we have to fight to get there.

It's in the fight we learn to become brave.

It's in the fight we learn we really can trust God.

It's in the fight we discover who we were created to be.

And as we fight, we must remember that God has equipped us for battle. "Because you have not been given the spirit of fear but of power, love, and a sound mind" (2 Timothy 1:7).

False Prophets and Catastrophizing

Erin became her own false prophet. By believing the lie and telling herself that the future was too scary to go down that road, she killed her business before it even got a chance to launch.

I've been a false prophet of negative, future situations time and time again in my life.

Remember the bowling class I dropped out of because I was sure the future scenarios in there were all terrible?

Another time I refused to put my oldest son (my most outgoing, social one) in a mother's-day-out program or preschool class because I was sure something bad would happen if he wasn't by my side every minute.

And before my book released to the world, remember how I pictured myself at yard sales, selling my book out of the trunk of my car for a quarter?

Experts in human behavior call this type of distortion in our thinking "catastrophizing." It's when we tell ourselves something bad is in the future and predict a catastrophe when there's no real evidence that anything bad will happen.

This happened to me several months ago as we were preparing to go visit my grandfather for the weekend. I have a sweet neighbor who comes over and checks on my dog, Mollie, three times a day when we're out of town. Mollie is well fed, goes on walks, and basically hangs out for a couple of days until we come home. Friday afternoon, as Mark was packing the minivan to leave for the weekend, I was walking Mollie to try to get her to use the bathroom before we left. She hadn't gone that morning and wasn't going that afternoon, and I got a little nervous.

I texted my two teenagers to ask them the last time Mollie had pooped. Jack reported back that she went on Wednesday. Well, it was Friday afternoon.

Within five minutes I went into full catastrophe mode. I started imagining all of the medical problems that could be wrong with my beloved dog. She was going to be home alone all weekend. What if she got sick and my neighbor had to take her to the vet? Mollie gets carsick; she'd throw up all over my neighbor's car. What if she had some sort of terrible blockage and died while we were gone and the neighbor found her? Or what if we came home Sunday night and my boys found her dead?

By this point full-blown catastrophizing was going on in my head.

Mollie and I marched up to Mark, who was still packing the minivan (bless him and his organized soul), and I gave him the news.

"Babe, I think I need to stay home this weekend. With Mollie."

"Why?"

"I'm pretty sure she has an intestinal blockage and if we leave her she might die."

"What's going on? Is her stomach distended? Is she not eating or drinking? How much is she throwing up?"

"Umm, none of that. I can't get her to poop."

"Since when?"

"Maybe Wednesday."

"Alli, we're going. She'll be fine. I promise."

I just needed a good reality check. I was marching in circles around my house catastrophizing the whole situation.

And guess what? She *was* fine.

Next time you find yourself catastrophizing the future, take a step back. Breathe deeply. Tell yourself you are imagining a worst-case scenario that probably won't even happen. And when necessary, submit yourself to a reality check from your spouse, a close friend, or someone else you trust to see the situation more clearly than you do.

We have to be careful that our concerns don't get blown up into catastrophes.

Emotions about the future can cloud our thinking, so in those times, we need to seek and find firm ground.

A Battle Plan to Fight Your Fear of the Future

No matter what obstacle and giant is looming in your future, no matter what fear the enemy has sent to take you out, I'm telling you that you can do it.

Greater is he who lives in us than he who lives in the world!

You can fight, and you will get through this.

Here's your battle plan.

1. Develop gratitude for what God is doing right now

We must make the decision to daily look for how God is providing in the present and develop gratitude. I want to be like the apostle Paul, who said, "I know what it is to be in need, and I know what it is to have plenty. I have learned the secret of being content in any and every situation, whether well fed or hungry, whether living in plenty or in want" (Philippians 4:14). But I'm so not like Paul. I'm restless, nervous about the future, and tend to have to talk myself off the proverbial ledge. So, to help me build that sense of contentment, I speak words of gratitude to God for what he is doing right now.

- *God, thank you that Mark hasn't had an asthma attack in twenty-four hours.*
- *God, thank you that my boys love you.*

155

- *God, thank you that you have opened doors for me to share what you are teaching me.*
- *God, thank you for the roof over my head.*
- *God, thank you for Nutella and Reese's Peanut Butter Cups.* (I have actually said that.)

Through gratitude, I'm learning to fight.

And so are you, my friend. So are you!

But the enemy wants us to think it's hopeless, that things will never get better, that there's no point in praying because what will happen will happen. To that you can say, "God, thank you that you have taught me the enemy is a liar!"

2. Think about your future self

Sometimes focusing on the future can actually help you. What do I mean? I mean picturing your future self and then making decisions today that will make your future self happy.

For example, "Future Alli" has made me get myself to bed on time. I'm a night owl by nature, but I lived for years where "Morning Alli" was ticked off at "Night Owl Alli" because she stayed up until after midnight and made me feel like I was run over by a truck the next day.

"Future Alli" has also saved me from procrastination. I've learned that if I spend just thirty minutes a day accomplishing things (those little oh-so-boring duties) I need to take care of, instead of putting them off because "I don't feel like it," then I can avoid setting myself up for failure in the future.

"Future Alli" helps with everything from the big decisions to the daily schedule.

"Future Alli" wants you to have this book in your hands, so "Today Alli" sits down at the computer and writes even when she'd rather watch a movie.

"Future Alli" wants a decent credit score, so "Today Alli" pays the bills on time.

"Future Alli" can be me in ten minutes, ten weeks, or even ten years. As in the examples above, the fact that I take a minute to think what my future self will think about something helps me reframe a decision I'm making, helping me take myself and my swirling emotions out of the present (or the past!) and think logically about the future.

3. Stack up your own stones of remembrance

We will always face new giants, and we will have lots of work to do cleaning out the brush of our own Promised Land. The struggles will come, the enemy will strike, and more and more giants will step onto our path as we live out our calling. In those times we can strengthen our faith by intentionally saving our stories, stacking up our own stones of remembrance.

I recently walked a friend through a valley season of her life as she watched her marriage crumble. Though it all looked hopeless, she stayed in the fight and fought hard for her marriage to be resurrected, and it was. As we talked about the pain she felt during the fight, and the pain she was feeling after, I told her to write it all down and to remember with gratitude all that God had done during that season. I asked her to document as much as she could, because the enemy never stops attacking, and one day she would need to be strengthened by remembering his faithfulness during this time.

Remembering what God has done in the past for you is the secret to finding strength for today's battles.

4. Ask the right questions

If you, like me, have a tendency to turn a concern into a catastrophe, it's important to have a strategy to overcome it. My strategy is to stop and ask what I call "right thinking" questions.

That's what Mark did for me in the situation with Mollie, when I was sure she was dying because she wouldn't go to the bathroom. I've learned to ask right thinking questions for myself. So when I feel like a situation is a catastrophe, I ask myself:

- How likely is this to happen?
- Is there any evidence this is a risk?
- Even if this is a risk, how much control do I actually have over the situation?

When you catch yourself catastrophizing, take a few minutes to pray, talk to a friend, and jot down your worries, looking at them with a detective's eyes. (See, all those episodes of Law and Order really are useful!)

5. Trust the master plan

God has a master plan for our lives. He has numbered our days. We have been chosen for this time in history, formed in our mother's womb, carefully created with certain gifts and talents for the life we have now and the life waiting for us in the future. The enemy comes to steal, kill, and destroy us by keeping us stuck, but we will fight back and take the land, even when it is filled with giants. We just have to trust his plan.

We can look forward to the future because God is already there.

As we face our future, the one God has mapped out for us, we can face it with hope. He knows who we are, he knows who he created us to be, and we aren't going to fall apart, because in his hands, in his plan, we don't have to fear the future.

Action Steps

Check out page 215 for your own space to practice your "right-thinking" skills.

- Think of a time when you felt attacked and fear of the future tried to keep you stuck in the wilderness. What methods did the enemy use to keep you afraid? When you know how the enemy has tried to hurt you in the past, you will be better prepared for battle in the future.

- Are you in a time of "in-between" or the "messy middle"? Pray that God gives you the ability to see the good around you, a profound sense of peace, and for strength to walk confidently into your future.

- Think of a time when God showed his faithfulness to you. How does that memory help reassure you about your future?

CHAPTER 10

WHAT IF I NEVER MEASURE UP?

Fear of Not Being Enough

I never imagined I would join a ministry. That is not how I saw myself. A wife? Yes. A mom? Yes. Entrepreneur? Yep. Someone who loves Jesus? You bet. Someone who works in a ministry? No way.

Ministry was for those who didn't skip over reading the more boring books of the Bible in their Bible reading plan (I'm looking at you, Leviticus), those who can stand up and give flowery prayers with poetic churchy words, and those who never forget to include others' prayer requests. That's who works in ministry.

Me? Not so much. I'm not flowery and poetic in my prayers. I get on my face and beg God, I grumble and complain to him, and I've been known to raise my face to the sky and yell at him. In my mind people in ministry are beautifully well-spoken and always do the right thing, whereas I'm stomping around like an angry child and taking advantage of the grace God gives so freely.

In the spring of 2014, when Christine Caine flew into Nashville, took me to dinner, and told me she wanted me to help her build Propel Women, I flat-out refused. I told her she was wrong, that I was not the girl for the job, and that Jesus would have to tell us both that this was a good idea because I thought it was a terrible one.

As it turns out, it was a good idea. Jesus had indeed called me to help build the ministry. And Christine laughed that it took me so long to hear from him. (In my defense, it was only a day and a half.) Here I was joining a global ministry, working with the same woman I had watched and learned from, from afar. Talk about exciting.

After just a few weeks, I presented Christine with a strategic plan, including the dates and information for Propel's first six, twelve, and eighteen months. Christine said, "That's great, but what does the Holy Spirit want us to do?"

I said, "I don't have a column for the Holy Spirit on my spread-sheet, Chris!"

Business plans, marketing strategies, brand positioning, product development—I have all of that covered. Making room and waiting for God to speak and move? Whoa. Nope. I realized I was out of my comfort zone.

A few months after starting my role as executive director of Propel Women, I attended a session at a conference where Christine was teaching. She gave a powerful talk, and as usual, her message made me want to, as she says so brilliantly, "charge hell with a water pistol." At the end of her talk, she announced, "If anyone here needs prayer, please come down to the front of the room. Members from my team will be here to pray with you and minister to you."

Umm . . . what?

The realization hit me that I was a member of her team, and I would be expected to be down there praying with people who came forward.

So I did what any mature, Christian woman would do. I went down to the front of the stage with Chris's team, but hid in the dark corner as far to one side of the stage as I could get, just hoping no one would see me and want me to pray with them. I let all the other team members comfort, pray over, and minister to the women in the crowd.

I mean, I can pray over myself. I can talk to God all day long, but who am I to minister to others? I can't do those poetic prayers!

I awkwardly watched team members pray over people and stood in the dark, praying that no one else would need anything. I thought over and over again, *I am not that girl. I am not that girl.*

One of the members of our team came up to me and said, "What are you doing? Get out of the shadows and go pray."

"Oh, no," I stammered. "I'm not great at ministering to people. I'm a business person. I need to leave that to people with that ministry gift."

He smiled kindly, put his hand on my shoulder, looked directly in my eyes, and said simply, "Alli, you *are* that girl."

His words were like an arrow in my heart, denouncing the lie I was speaking over myself.

His words were the simple reminder I needed to stop focusing on myself and what I believed I couldn't do, what I believed I wasn't good enough to do, and instead start focusing on what I was *called* to do.

The enemy wanted me to believe his lie in order to keep me from living out my calling that day. But isn't that the way he works?

The enemy whispers, "You're not good enough to follow God's calling in your life.

"You aren't good enough to serve and help others."

"You aren't equipped to build that business."

"You aren't smart enough to pursue your God-given dreams."

"You aren't strong enough to walk through a tough season with grace."

"You aren't lovable enough to be completely loved and accepted by others."

We are in a war, a war for our hearts and our minds. Even though our souls are safe and protected by Jesus, the enemy battles every day to get into our hearts and our minds.

We internalize his lies as truth and tell ourselves the same lies the enemy is speaking over us. When this happens, we are joining the enemy and doing his work for him.

The Screwtape Letters Game

One of my very favorite books is *The Screwtape Letters* by C. S. Lewis. It's a quick read, and I've read it about twenty-five times. It is a series of letters written from the perspective of the devil, who is writing to his understudy devil about how to destroy the life of a Christian convert. I think I've learned more about human nature and just how insidious spiritual warfare is from that book than I have from all other books about spiritual warfare I've read since.

Lewis's entire book reminds the reader to remember the devil is a liar. In other words, lying is what the devil does, and he has been practicing this evil art since the Garden of Eden!

My husband and I play what we call the Screwtape Letters game inspired by the book. When we are going through a big transition, a tough time, or just the daily grind, one of us will ask the other, "If I were the enemy, what three ways would I try to hurt me in this situation? How would I try to take me out? What lies would I tell me; what distractions would I use to derail me; what thoughts would I use to confuse me?"

And you want to know what's amazing? We can almost always hit the nail on the head. Many times when Mark has asked me that question, I have quickly popped out three tactics of the enemy, and then realized those are the exact three things I've been thinking or feeling.

For example: I was asked to come to my children's school to talk to the middle school girls. If you don't have much experience giving talks to middle schoolers, let me tell you now, they are a tough crowd. Not only do they not give you any positive feedback, it's like that middle school awkwardness just oozes from them and leaps out onto you. (As a speaker, there's nothing harder than pouring your heart out to people who look at you like they don't want to be there. It really is the worst.)

I was scared and nervous about talking to all these middle school girls, and I couldn't figure out why. So Mark played the Screwtape Letters game with me. I quickly thought of three ways the enemy could try to hurt me in this situation.

He would say, "You have boys. You know nothing about middle school girls."

And he would say, "You can't help them; these girls don't want to listen to anything you say."

And finally, the worst (and most effective lie of all): "You're just going to embarrass your sons."

Mark and I laughed, because you can quickly spot the absurdity of the statements as you play this game. But here's the crazy thing: in the twenty-four hour period before I went in to talk with those girls, every one of those statements filled my head at random times. But because I was aware that there was a battle going on, and that I am empowered to take every thought captive, I didn't have to waste any of my time being upset with the enemy's lies. I readily dismissed them.

When we are aware of the enemy's attack plan, we can win the battle.

I walked into that room and poured my heart out to those sweet middle school girls, because I kept myself focused on the fact that I was there to help them, and I did not take time to worry about shortcomings.

I shared the Screwtape Letters game with a friend of mine recently who struggles with rejection, and she shared her game results with me. She was looking on Facebook (Seriously, how many times do bad stories start with that phrase?), and she noticed that her friend's daughter had received an award for having good character. Immediately she felt envious of both her friend and her friend's daughter. So she asked herself, "If the enemy was going to try to get to me right now, what would he be saying?"

He might say, "Your friend is such a great parent. Too bad you aren't as good a mom as she is."

Or he might say, "Her daughter gets every single award. It's because her family can afford all those extracurricular activities."

Or he would say, "Aren't you embarrassed your daughters never get awards like that?"

She told me when she played the Screwtape Letters game she realized those were the exact thoughts she was having. She said, "None of those things are true. I'm proud of my friend and her daughter. It's great to see positive things getting attention these days!"

There is real power in stepping back for just a minute and looking at things from a new perspective.

Taking Away the Enemy's Power

Let's go back to that moment where all my insecurities and feelings of unworthiness converged and I found myself hiding in a dark corner instead of serving women who needed prayer.

What if I played the game in that situation too? How was the enemy trying to keep me from doing what I was called to do in that moment?

By telling me I wasn't good enough to minister to others.

By telling me that I didn't know how to pray well, and that

the other person would judge me and my praying skills (as if there is such a thing as praying skills. How silly is that?).

By telling me that someone with a past like mine (full of mistakes and years spent running away from what God wanted for my life) can't dare to claim the name of Jesus and think themselves good enough to pray over people.

You see how sinister seeds of doubt are? They grow into weeds, then take hold in our lives and choke out what God is calling us to accomplish in his name.

Before we know it, we have picked up the tools of the enemy and turned them on ourselves. And many of us do his job, continually doing the enemy's work for him every day. We do this by the way we talk to ourselves. The words we use against ourselves are almost always more painful than those of anyone else.

If we allow those seeds of doubt to go unchecked, they will sprout up into weeds of insecurity, confusion, and fear. We cannot just keep chopping off the top of the weeds, hoping they won't crop up again. We have to get to the root of them and rip them out of there.

When we step back and say, "If I were the enemy, how would I try to stop me?" it takes the devil's power away. And it reminds us to see ourselves and our situation through the eyes of Jesus.

Seeing Ourselves through the Eyes of Jesus

When we become Christians, Jesus accepts us, all of us, including our selfish ways, our anger, our insecurities, and our fears. He takes it all and accepts us completely. He wipes away our past guilt and not only offers us salvation for our afterlife, but acceptance in our present life. He starts with wherever we are, but he doesn't just leave us there. He moves us forward to whatever next step we need to take.

Let's look again at Jesus's encounter with the Samaritan woman at the well, recorded in John 4. While we tend to marvel at her list of mistakes—married five times and now living in sin!—Jesus treats them almost matter-of-factly. He knows who she is. What he's more interested in is: does she know who *he* is? And once she does know who he is, she can't help but be transformed!

We often don't accept ourselves in the moment. Even after we become Christians, we stumble and bumble and fall, and instead of keeping our eyes on Jesus and who he is and what he's done for us, we get self-conscious and self-critical and self-blaming. That's why the discipline of practicing godly self-acceptance instead of indulging in sinful self-criticism is crucial to our life and our happiness.

When we allow ourselves to be self-critical and beat ourselves up over our present or past mistakes, we are doing the enemy's job for him. We call ourselves Christians because Christ redeemed us. But we live like we don't really believe that what he did on the cross was enough to redeem us.

We refuse to trust God's love enough to heal our ugliest thoughts, to change our worst behaviors, and to soothe our most troubling emotions. Why? Because maybe, just maybe, at our core, we feel his promise of restoration, redemption, and total recovery is for others who aren't as messed up inside as we think we are.

> Our restoration, redemption, and recovery can only come when we keep our eyes fixed on Jesus.

When we don't offer ourselves to Jesus at our most broken, we stay stuck in our pain, and we don't believe his promise of healing or feel his presence. We have to believe down to our core that we are loved and accepted by Jesus. In our minds, we know what the Bible says, that in Christ we are made whole.

But we live like we believe that's not true.

What would life look like if we walked in the belief that we are truly, madly, deeply loved and accepted, just as we are, and not as we think we should be?

None of us has fully grasped who Jesus is or who he's called us to be. Even Paul admits it's a process. He moans, "I do not understand what I do. For what I want to do I do not do, but what I hate I do" (Romans 7:15).

You are reading this for a reason. God wants you to stop doing the enemy's work for him.

This book is your battle plan to fight back.

The enemy lies to us and tells us that we're not enough, that our worth is based on something other than who we are created to be in Christ. He lies and tells us that we don't measure up, that our worth is tied to our performance. He tells us to judge our value based on how we compare to others, that it is not enough to do well; we have to be the best. It's not enough to do a good job; we have to do the *best* job.

> Whatever God calls you to do, he will strengthen you to do.

Let me tell you something today. Jesus takes our mess and makes it his best. We don't have to be "good enough," because he has already declared us perfect. Whatever he called you to do in this world, he has in all his vast wisdom judged you to be worthy. And through the empowerment of the Holy Spirit in you, you will be equipped for all you are meant to do (Hebrews 13:21). With this truth and this power, we are free to be brave, strong, and secure.

If God, maker of all heaven and earth, has complete confidence in us, who are we to doubt ourselves?

All we have to do is press forward to win the prize he's already claimed for us.

Slow of Speech and Terrified

Moses was a man who knew all about feeling insecure and not good enough. There he was, a stuttering murderer-turned-sheep-herder, in the middle of the desert, hiding from the law, when God spoke to him from the burning bush and told him he was going to use him to free the Hebrew nation from bondage.

Moses's first response is a lot like my first response to anything hard, when I find reasons to back up my position that *I'm not that girl!* Moses took one look at God's plan and immediately protested: "Who am I that I should go to Pharaoh and bring the Israelites out of Egypt?" (Exodus 3:11). In other words, "Hey, God, I'm not that guy!"

God, being God, reminded Moses it wasn't about him or what he could do in his own power. He said, "I will be with you. And this will be the sign to you that it is I who have sent you: When you have brought the people out of Egypt, you will worship God on this mountain" (Exodus 3:12).

But still, that wasn't enough for Moses. He then asked God for his name so he could be sure to tell Pharaoh who was sending him. Then Moses, once again, focused on himself and all his fears and the reasons why he was not the right guy for the job.

"What if they don't believe me?" (Exodus 4:1).

"I can't speak well" (Exodus 4:10).

"I am slow of speech!" (Exodus 4:10).

God reminded Moses that he not only created humans, but he made Moses's mouth. He would give Moses the words to say. "I brought you into this world. I am pretty sure I can put words into your mouth when I need to." (Maybe it didn't happen exactly like that, but I like to picture it in my head that way!)

God went on to tell Moses all the signs he would provide to prove to Pharaoh that God had sent him.

His staff would turn into a snake (Exodus 4:3–5).

His hand would turn white with leprosy and then be healed as he essentially played peekaboo with his jacket (Exodus 4:6–7).

And if that wasn't enough, he would turn water into blood (Exodus 4:8–9).

And still, after all that, Moses's fear and intimidation still caused him to focus on himself and not on God. He said, "Send someone else" (Exodus 4:13).

God got mad (as a parent, I totally get this) but was merciful and said, "Okay, you can take Aaron with you because you are so scared, and I'll give you both the words to say" (Exodus 4:14–17).

Moses had to learn to see himself through God's eyes. Once we learn to see ourselves as God sees us, we can see ourselves as enough. Because we will learn that we are not operating under our own power, but in God's strength.

The Bible is filled with people who didn't believe they had what it took to live up to God's calling. Isaiah, Jacob, Noah, Mary the mother of Jesus, Joseph, Zacchaeus, and Paul (to name a few) all were called by God for a specific purpose, and all felt certain God was calling the wrong person. They, like Moses, were too hard on themselves and believed the lie that they weren't good enough to be used by God.

God always calls people who aren't perfect, people who don't measure up, people who make mistakes and fall. It's what he does! The fact that we as such flawed and fallible people stay committed to listening to his voice, obeying his commands, and staying close to him shows the power of the Spirit of Christ in us empowering us to do all he calls us to do, be all he created us to be, and live bravely in this crazy world.

Are You Too Hard on Yourself?

Are you like Moses and these other great people of the Bible, believing that you don't have what it takes to be used by God? I sure was (and sometimes still am). Here are a few ways to recognize if you are too hard on yourself.

1. Do you feel guilty when you relax?

We live in a culture that constantly tells us that we are not good enough. It's impossible to not internalize some of the hundreds of messages that come at us each day.

If, when you relax and try to enjoy life in the present, you catch yourself thinking that you should be doing something else, achieving more, working more, exercising more, cleaning more, serving more, maybe it's time to simply give yourself permission to be. To rest.

What would it look like in your life if you gave yourself permission to rest and recharge?

2. Do you talk to yourself in a way you wouldn't talk to others?

Here's a truth that took me thirty years to learn: the only person who spends her day judging you or criticizing you is *you*. Your worst enemy is your own critical voice in your head. This is the voice you listen to ten times more than any other. The constant thoughts that you aren't good enough, that you've failed once again, and that things will never be better will steal your passion and your joy. Learning to silence, or at least ignore, the critical inner voice is key to your happiness.

A friend once challenged me and some friends to observe how we were speaking to ourselves for a week and ask ourselves these questions:

Would I say something so hateful to a person I love?

When has stressing out about a mistake ever made me feel better about myself?

After I spent time looking at how I was talking to myself, I realized that I was not only being terrible to myself, but I also realized God probably wasn't happy with how I was speaking to his daughter either.

As I've said before in earlier chapters (because we need the reminder again and again), how might your life be different if you only spoke to yourself with self-compassion instead of self-criticism?

3. Do you expect perfection from yourself?

I believe all of us who want to do things with excellence have a tendency to fall into the perfectionist trap. Here are some questions that can help you recognize if you're being a little too hard on yourself because of perfectionism.

- Do you ever worry about things not being good enough so you stay stuck and don't take action? Sometimes this happens because you believe everything has to be done a certain way or it's not worth doing.
- Do you worry that you aren't doing a good job and focus on your mistakes after the fact?
- Are you harder on yourself than you are others?
- Do you ever get depressed when you don't do something the way it was supposed to be done?

What I've learned is that no one feels completely capable and no one has unlimited funds, time, and energy to do everything they want to do in life. And everyone is terrified of failure, looking foolish, and letting others down. But for those of us with perfectionistic tendencies, these fears can keep us stuck.

> We can't let our desire for perfection become procrastination.

The way I've learned to manage this on a day-to-day basis is to ask myself, *Am I striving for excellence or demanding perfection?* Excellence is a worthy goal that energizes and inspires; perfectionism wraps us in guilt and gets us nowhere.

What would it look like if you gave yourself
grace and said good enough is perfect?

4. Do you suffer from imposter syndrome?

If you have imposter syndrome it means you feel like a fraud because despite your accomplishments, you believe you aren't really smart, capable, creative, or deserving no matter what you have achieved in life.

My favorite example of imposter syndrome is from Maya Angelou: "Each time I write a book, every time I face that yellow pad, the challenge is so great. I have written eleven books, but each time I think, 'Uh oh, they're going to find out now. I've run a game on everybody and they're going to find me out.'"[1]

Despite all the success we have in our lives, deep down inside, we still judge ourselves to be undeserving. We worry that at any moment the world will realize we have no idea what we are doing.

What would it look like in your life if every time you felt like a fraud, you recognized the feeling as a normal part of the journey, and not an indication that you don't measure up?

5. Do you beat yourself up over things that are out of your control?

I know there are some things you need to stop brooding over and beating yourself up about right now. (Don't ask me how I know. I just know.) Let's dive in.

You hate the way you look. God made you. He designed you to be a certain height, with a certain type of hair, a special nose, and even with a certain shaped pinky fingernail. The enemy is a master of distracting and hurting women of God by keeping us busy hating how we look. No one, and I mean *no one*, is out there preoccupied with your appearance and judging your looks. I promise. You look wonderful.

And on days you feel like you aren't looking amazing, just stay off the Internet. You'll thank me later.

You're frustrated with your season of life. For some reason everyone is programmed with this thinking that we will be happy in the future. Once we reach a certain goal then we will feel great, we'll have meaning, and all will be glorious. When you're in college, you think you'll be happy when you get that degree. After you get that degree, you think you'll be happy when you get that job. Once you get that job, you think you'll be happy when you're married. When you get married, you think you'll be happy when you finally have that baby. When you have that baby, you think you'll finally be happy when the baby can sleep through the night (actually, when *you* can sleep through the night). And on, and on, and on.

When we constantly put off our own happiness and judge our current season of life as just a stepping stone to the next success point, we are left unhappy with the present.

And when we're unhappy with our present, that's when we beat ourselves up and blame ourselves for life not being good enough yet. Who we are and where we are just never is *enough*.

You are disgusted and dismayed by your past. Your past is over. But when you allow yourself to brood over your past mistakes and continually punish yourself for them, you pollute the present with the past.

As Christians, we have the gift of the clean slate. Through the process of repenting (which in layperson's terms just means feeling genuinely **Don't pollute your present with the poison of your past.** remorseful for what you've done and turning away from it) and asking for forgiveness from Jesus, we are set free from our past.

What would it look like for you to stop being so hard on

yourself? To accept that you are who you are, that you are where you should be, and that your past is in the past?

6. Do you think that everyone is secretly judging you?

When we are hard on ourselves, a little lens in our brain assumes everyone thinks of us negatively as well. We beat ourselves up, and we can't imagine other people not judging us just like we judge ourselves. And sadly, if we are too self-critical, we can end up sabotaging the close and supportive relationships we crave.

This is why, with our loved ones and our best girlfriends, we can be so easily hurt and offended. It's because what we say to ourselves becomes the filter we see the world through.

What would life look like if you decided to treat yourself like Jesus treats you? What if you told yourself, "Do not let your heart be troubled. Believe in Jesus!" (John 14:1).

A Battle Plan to Fight the Fear of Not Being Enough

On some days it may be enough to tell ourselves that in Christ, we are enough, and to say that we know God sees us as perfect. But on the days when it feels easier to believe the lies of the enemy, it's important for us to have a battle plan.

1. Dig deep into how much God loves you

When I sang the song "No Longer Slaves," I thought about the lyrics in a new way. I was no longer a slave to fear, and then the very next line reminded me that I am a child of God. As I sang those two sentences over and over again, over myself, they became an anthem.

I am a child of God.

"See what great love the Father has lavished on us, that we should be called children of God! And that is what we are!" (1 John 3:1)

As a mom, I know that I will never experience a stronger, more pure love than the love I have for my children. Because they know how much I love them, and are secure that nothing they can do will ever cause me to stop loving them, turn away from them, or stop caring for them, they have a comfort with me, a boldness (that sometimes is a little too bold), and a deep security.

Not until I became a mother could I wrap my brain around how powerful that love is. I don't think to this day I can fully grasp how much God loves us as his beloved children. But I try!

2. Surround yourself with supportive people

You need to be around friends with whom you can be vulnerable *and who accept you as you are.*

The people you surround yourself with can build you up or tear you down. With each year that passes I appreciate my girlfriends who know me, accept me, and love me even at my ugliest (inside and out).

When I'm fighting intimidation, insecurity, and all around feeling not good enough, my best girlfriends play a key role in helping me see straight and encouraging me to get out of the pit.

Nurture the relationships that nurture you.

Through the years I noticed that certain friends would jokingly put me down so that when I left a visit with them, I always felt slightly worse than I did before I met with them. Instead of building me up, those relationships were tearing me down. So I made the tough decision at the time to drop those friends and instead spend time nurturing the relationships that nurtured me. And let me tell you this, it was hard at the time to drop the friendships, but now I look back and wonder what took me so long!

3. Celebrate who made you and what makes you wonderful

You may not know this, you may not accept this (that is your choice), but you are wonderful. I believe with all my heart that you are reading this book not by accident, not by chance, but to be reminded that you are created to fight back fear, to love well, and to embrace the fact that you were created by a God who delights in you. Delights. In. You.

There's something about being a Christian woman that makes us a little uncomfortable even thinking about how wonderful we are. I mean, that's not humble, right?

True humility is not thinking less of ourselves, but thinking of ourselves less.

Somewhere along the way we believed the lie that we are supposed to think we are the dirt, not the beautiful flowers that grow up out of it.

You are fearfully and wonderfully made. Knitted in your mother's womb for a purpose. You are not a cosmic accident. You are beautiful.

There is real strength and power in learning to carry ourselves with both humility and godly confidence as women of God.

4. Remember that growth is a process that takes faith and time

So often our fears of not being enough are based in a deep distrust of God and how he works. We want things *here*, we want things *now*, and we don't want to go through the messy growth process of traveling from here to there over a long period of time. It is very easy to lose perspective, get impatient, and allow the fear of not being enough to become an excuse to not trust God with the next step. If we aren't careful, we can go from thinking *we* aren't enough to thinking *he* isn't enough to make us better. For each of us to truly be all God has called us to be, we have to stop focusing on what we don't have and where we've messed up, and instead learn to focus on where he is taking us, how he is growing us, and who he is refining us to be.

To be sure, growth isn't instantaneous. It takes time, and faith, and yes, some blood, sweat, and tears. Jesus is still writing our story.

So in some ways, yes, let's admit it. We don't measure up. We're not enough. We haven't attained our goal. We're not there yet. But we know that the good work he has begun in us, he will finish. And *Jesus* is enough. *Jesus* is there at the finish line. Because *Jesus* is the goal.

So let's press on. Our prize is just ahead!

Action Steps

Identify a lie the enemy has spoken to you that you tell yourself as part of your story. Use the tool on page 216 to write the lies he has tried to hurt you with and replace them with the truth.

- Take a certain situation you are facing right now and play the Screwtape Letters game. Ask yourself: "If I were the enemy, what three things would I say to derail me?" Go to page 217 for a place to write your answers.
- Go to page 218 and ask yourself the five questions to determine if you are too hard on yourself. If you answer three or more with *yes*, it's time to give yourself some self-compassion.
- Reread the battle plan for overcoming the fear of not being enough. Which steps can you start doing today?

CHAPTER 11

WHAT IF I CAN'T TRUST GOD?

Fear that We Are on Our Own

Early in our marriage, when our boys were much younger, Mark and I moved often for his career. I didn't enjoy moving, though I tried to make the best of it. Looking back, I can see I was worried about the future and whether our kids might not be okay, but at the time, all I knew was that I was stressed out. And my response to stress was to clamp down and try to control as much as I could.

Each time we moved, I researched every single neighborhood within a twenty-mile radius of Mark's work. I read everything I could get my hands on and questioned real estate agents like their lives (or ours) depended on it. When I found a house I thought was the right one, I drove through the neighborhood at various times of day just to be sure I knew what the neighborhood was really like. One time I even chased down a kid on a bike to ask him what he knew about the neighbors! (Yes, I know that's weird and would probably get me arrested these days, but kids have the best intel!)

As the boys grew older, I homeschooled them because there was no way I could send them off to a new school in a new city every time we moved. There were too many variables in that scenario. Too many things that could go wrong. Too many situations outside of my control.

Then our lives pivoted, and I became the working parent. You have no idea the pressure I put on Mark to parent like I parented, clean like I cleaned (men don't have the same definition of clean as women do, ahem), cook like I cooked (who am I kidding? He's a way better cook than I am!). I knew I had to release "home" to Mark, so I did the only thing I could do: I controlled my work life.

My event and marketing company allowed me to channel my controlling tendencies in a new way. I liked to think of myself as conscientious, but I'm sure I made people crazy asking for constant details and updates on upcoming events. I made it *my* job to be sure they did *their* job.

One day, as we were preparing for the upcoming BlissDom Women's Conference, I had pushed one of our team members to the breaking point. My best friend, Megan (yes, the same Megan who talked me down off my FOMO ledge) worked for me. She took me into an office and gave me some "real talk." "Alli, I know you think you are being conscientious, but you aren't. You are just being controlling. You are basically saying, 'I don't trust anyone to handle this the right way, so I'm going to make sure you do every single thing my way.'"

Megan's words hit me hard. My need to control was really a lack of trust, and I realized that lack of trust was present in every area of my life. I didn't trust my teammates to do their jobs "correctly." I didn't trust my husband to parent "the right way." I didn't trust the schools to teach "properly." I didn't trust the real estate agents to point us to "the right" neighborhoods.

As I traced that line of thought as far back as I could, I realized I didn't actually trust anyone but myself, and that's when I remembered something a friend had said just a few months earlier.

"If you live your daily life depending on yourself, and never truly humbling yourself and submitting to God, you are no different than the agnostic who doesn't really believe in God."

In an instant I was stopped in my tracks. I had been working so hard to be a good wife, good mom, and good business owner that I had essentially stopped believing that I needed to trust in Jesus.

I was busy trusting in Alli.

I was happily controlling everything, moving the pieces around in my own little game of Life.

But I was behaving that way—controlling every detail on my own—because in my heart I didn't believe Jesus really cared about the details of my life, nor could I count on him to come through for me when it really mattered. After all, my dad died when I was just a kid. Why didn't God stop that? And Mark and I lost everything we owned when the economy tanked. Why didn't God step in and prevent that?

Sure, I knew God loved me. I read the Bible. I sang the song in Sunday school, "Jesus loves me this I know, for the Bible tells me so." And of course I knew I could depend on him to save me from hell and secure my place for eternity in heaven.

But depend on him in the day-to-day? That was not how I was living.

For weeks after Megan called me out about being controlling, I looked at my behavior. Sure enough, I gave Jesus lots of lip service, I said all the right things, I did my quick prayers, but I didn't trust him with the details. My own controlling actions were a glaring testimony to my lack of trust.

How We See God

I went to see a good friend, who is also a counselor, to help me unpack the what's and the why's of my heart and my behavior through the years. She helped me understand that for many Christians, our view of God is tinted by how we feel about our earthly fathers.

My father died in a tragic car accident when I was almost three. My mom always made it a point to tell me how much my father loved me. She showed me photos of me in my dad's loving arms. I never ever, one time, doubted that my father loved me. In fact, I *knew* he loved me. His love for me was deeply woven into my heart.

However, when I was hurt, there were no strong arms I could be held in. There was no security when I called out for Daddy.

There was just disappointment.

Even though my dad had no control over his death, even though he didn't *want* to leave me, all I knew as a young girl was that he wasn't there.

And subconsciously, I carried that view of my father to God the Father.

I believed that God loved me. I believed that he was good and wanted good for me.

But my actions showed that I didn't really believe I could trust him. I didn't believe I could count on him to be around when I needed him most.

I was loved, but I was on my own to figure out life, both physically and spiritually.

I shared a bit about this realization in *Breaking Busy*, and so many women wrote to me and shared that their early experiences with their own earthly fathers also clouded their view of God, the Father.

A sweet woman emailed me and shared she viewed God as a manipulative puppet master because her parents were so controlling. She realized she'd never really wanted to give up control to God because giving up control (in her life experience) meant she wasn't safe anymore.

In one heartbreaking email another woman shared the story of growing up in a home with abuse, and then her father rejecting her, her brother, and her mother, and walking away from the family when she was eight. She never saw her father again and was left with a huge wound. She said, "I still struggle with believing I can trust God. Not only can I not say the word *father* without feeling pain, I wrestle with why God let my father abuse and then abandon us."

One of my best friends told me that she struggles to trust God because in her core she feels that God is disappointed with her. It wasn't until she made the connection between her relationship with her parents and her view of God that she realized that her hypercritical parents left her feeling like she was a disappointment and a failure. It was easy for her to transfer that view onto God as well.

Positive experiences with our fathers, on the other hand, can help us experience God's goodness. Another woman shared that she was so grateful that her dad was so loving and always trustworthy because it helped her to understand the deep love of God. For her, trusting God was instinctual because of her relationship with her dad.

I think it's very important for all of us to take the time to ask the Holy Spirit to reveal to us if our earlier experiences have affected our view of God and our ability to trust him.

I have also discovered that beyond how I think of God as a Father, I also apply other life circumstances to the character of God.

For example, when God didn't stop us from losing everything, I felt I couldn't trust him as our "provider." When he didn't heal Mark in our time frame, I couldn't trust him as our "healer."

Over time, I had built up quite a case against God as being worthy of my trust. (How's that for a true confession?)

If you're like me, you too may have built a case to prove that God is not worthy to be trusted. You know how I know this? Because it is a particularly effective tool of the enemy.

The enemy is going to try to get us to see God in the way that will wound us the most.

If your wound is that your earthly father deserted you (even through death), then the enemy is going to try to have you view God through that lens and declare

The enemy uses our wounds to distort our view of God.

him God-the-deserter. If your wound is that someone you love wasn't healed this side of heaven, then you are going to view God through that lens, God-who-doesn't-heal. If your wound is that someone on this earth rejected you, then you are going to view God through that lens, God-the-rejector.

The enemy wants us to believe the lie that we can't trust God, and he uses our past hurts and disappointments to cloud our view of God and convince us we can't rely on him.

How the Enemy Tries to Keep Us from Trusting God

The enemy sows seeds of mistrust. He attacks our peace and happiness from every angle and tries to steal the security and acceptance we enjoy in Christ. He is the mastermind of the five Bad B's and uses them to try to keep us from trusting God.

- He wants us to stay *busy* and not think about God.
- He wants us to *blame* God for anything that goes wrong in our lives.
- He wants us to *bury* and deny we even have an issue trusting God.
- He wants us to *binge* on the opinions of others, on food, on TV, and on the internet instead of bingeing on the Word or time with God.
- He wants us to *brood* fearfully over every important situation.

186

was literally *in* the boat, and yet they were sure they were going to die. They felt certain he was going to sleep right through the shipwreck of their lives.

I've been there. Wanting God to tell me every step of the way what to do. Wanting him to step in and steady the sail, stay at the helm, and encourage me to stay strong. But instead I hear him say, "Do not fear, I am with you."

And yet even with me hearing his reassurance, in those moments I have wanted to say, "Jesus, are you sleeping through this storm right now? Can't you see I'm drowning here?"

During our dark days, it's easy to feel like we are drowning and Jesus is sleeping through our shipwreck.

So what did Jesus do when the disciples woke him up and announced that they were all going to die? He woke up and fussed at them, that's what he did!

He doesn't give them all a bear hug and comfort them. He doesn't hold their hands and give them a pep talk either.

Nope. He gets up, tells the storm to chill out, *and it obeys.* And then, once he's whipped the storm into shape, he turns around and says, "Why are you all afraid? Do you still have no faith?" (Mark 4:39–40).

You know he had to be thinking, *I am literally right here with you in this boat!*

You can trust your Savior with your storm.

The storms of life sometimes show us our own lack of trust. Storms in my life have shown me that it's easy to proclaim my trust when the seas are smooth and I feel in control, but when I find myself gasping for air and trying to keep my feet under me, my lack of trust becomes pretty apparent.

A sweet friend of mine shared her story of how the enemy convinced her that she couldn't trust God in the middle of her storm.

The enemy attacks best when we are in our hardest seasons—in the storms of life—times of pain, fear, and loneliness.

But we gain trust by going to God in the middle of our storms, and crying out to the one who has promised us that his grace is sufficient. Without our struggles in the storms, would we ever really learn to trust him?

I realized recently how contradictory my prayers for my sons are. I pray that they grow to be great men of God, that they have a profound sense of purpose, and that they love and trust God. However, I also pray that they never have to endure suffering or struggles, because oh, how I hate to see them hurting! Yet how are they going to learn to trust God if they never experience a time when only God can help them?

In the Storms

I believe it is *in the storms* that we learn to trust, to stay strong, to fight.

Sure, when I'm in the storm all I can see is the lightning, all I can hear is the wind, and all I can feel are the waves crashing against me. But I have also learned that when the storm is over, one of two things will be true. The storm will have actually been the death of me, and I'll wake up in heaven (Yay! Heaven!). Or (and this is more likely the case), I will see the sunlight on the other side of the storm. And I'll keep my eyes on the light until I'm out of the storm. Then I will look back, and I will say, "Whew, I didn't die after all."

In the storms of life we learn to trust, stay strong, and fight.

Each time I look back at the storms in my life, I see so clearly how God was teaching me, how Jesus was guiding me, and how the Holy Spirit was comforting me.

When Mark and I lost everything, I remember lying in bed with him (a grown-up, with kids, living at my granddaddy's house because we were broke) and thinking we wouldn't survive. But we did survive. And we thrived. And God showed us that putting our faith in material objects (and having to strive so hard to keep up with all of it) was not what he wanted for our lives.

He allowed us to make a wreck of our lives, and he then rescued us from the mess we had made for ourselves.

When I was agonizing over whether or not to leave BlissDom, Jesus was there guiding me in a journey to trust him. I didn't know what was next for me professionally; all I knew was I had to decide I wanted what *Jesus* wanted for me more than what *I* wanted.

And when Mark was so sick and I worried that he might never get well, I felt the comfort of the Holy Spirit reassuring me that there was hope, and that I could rest in the reassurance that God was in control. I also learned during that time that sometimes when you *know* things are out of your control, you actually feel better realizing you don't have to try to be in control.

But you better believe I had very little insight in the middle of those storms.

In the middle of my stormy seasons, my pain, fear, confusion, and pride all worked together to blind me to God's work in me and in the situations around me.

It's in those storms that the enemy comes to plant the seeds of mistrust. Then he waters those seeds with lies until they grow into weeds—the fear we feel, the panic we get attacked by, and the constant state of worry we live with.

It's in the stormy seasons that you learn just how weak you are. But thank God, it's also when you learn just how powerful God is.

Asleep at the Helm

Sometimes when storms come they can show us that we may *say* we trust God, but we don't actually believe he is with us or cares enough to help us. This happened to the disciples.

One night, as Jesus and his disciples were crossing the Sea of Galilee, a storm hit. (Mark 4:35–41) The Sea of Galilee is over six hundred feet below sea level, and it is surrounded by cliffs that are over two thousand feet tall. When the wind hits just right, the storms are apparently quite horrific, and the sea swirls as the winds hit those tall cliff faces. And even though the disciples were seasoned fishermen, they were terrified and helpless in the face of this violent storm.

So what did Jesus do? Did he spring into action and calmly tell the disciples how to steady the ship? Did he assume the role of captain, barking out orders and calming everyone's fears?

Nope. Jesus was napping. Asleep. Just chilling on a pillow.

Can you even imagine the disciples' confusion and frustration? Jesus had checked out, possibly when they needed him more than they ever had before.

The fear and frustration grew stronger until finally, terrified and probably a little ticked off, they woke him up and said, "Teacher, don't you care if we drown?"

They thought they were dying and that Jesus not only couldn't save them, but that he didn't *care* if they all died.

How many times in our lives do we feel like we are about to drown in our pain and fear? And not only does Jesus not magically make it all better, we also fear that he doesn't care at all.

Remember how in the middle of my darkest months I cried out to him and heard only these words over and over, "I am with you," and how frustrated that left me?

Jesus was physically there with the disciples on that boat. He

For months after my ex-husband left, I was terrified of getting a divorce. I was paralyzed at the thought of signing the papers. Why? Because I was scared of going to hell.

Literally. I was terrified of burning in hell because I got a divorce.

The kids and I came home one night from ball practice to letters he had written to each of us. He had left, moved a thousand miles away from the kids and me "to go find himself." He filed for divorce and there I was—scared out of my mind. It wasn't the finances. I had been the only one working the last year. It wasn't "my kids are going to be so screwed up"—the environment was so unhealthy to begin with, it couldn't be any worse.

I was just crazy scared of how much God was going to hate me and never let me into heaven.

That still sounds so juvenile to even think now. Because I, of all people, have known my entire life that there is nothing we can do to lose the love of the Lord. He loves us in our messiest messes. But that irrational fear paralyzed me for months. Finally, I was able to really hear the wisdom of those God had placed in the boat with me, the people there to reassure me, "He loves me. He will never leave me."

Maybe because I was already feeling the ultimate rejection from my husband of twenty years, it was easy to believe that even God could reject me and deny me. Nothing could be further from the truth. And I am so thankful for those friends he placed there alongside me. I was so scared of him and what he thought of me during that time, I had completely forgotten to trust him. He has carried me through the worst of seasons—and divorce was just the tip of the iceberg. I was left with no other choice but to trust him.

And as always, he delivered. Yes, I've remarried. That was just a bonus. But prior to finding my husband, the Lord delivered peace into my life. A confidence I've never known. And a true joy for life in the messiest of storms.

When a fear gets in us, it can overtake every little thought and cause every level of self-doubt in life.

The enemy attacked my friend with fear in the middle of her storm, and she briefly lost sight of the truth that we can trust God, that he is good, and his love will never fail us.

I love her story. I especially love the part about God placing other people in her boat to ride out the storm with her, reassuring her along the way. Sometimes we can lose sight of God's genuine concern for us, and when that happens, find it easy to believe we cannot trust him. When that happens, we need to turn to remind ourselves—and be reminded—of who God is.

Why Can We Trust God?

Trusting God is a process. Unfortunately, as we have learned, the only way to trust God is from experiences that require us to *need* to trust him.

A wonderful (and less painful) additional way to learn to trust God is to get to know him, to know who he is, his heart, and his nature. And we find those things out about him by reading Scripture.

Who is God? The Bible says:

- God lavishes us with love. "How great is the love the father has lavished on us that we should be called the children of God" (1 John 3:1).
- God is all-knowing. "God is greater than our hearts, and he knows everything" (1 John 3:20).
- God is loving and wants only good for us. "But you, O Lord, are a God merciful and gracious, slow to anger and abounding in steadfast love and faithfulness" (Psalm 86:15).

- God works things out for our good. "And we know that in all things God works for the good of those who love him, who have been called according to his purpose" (Romans 8:28).
- God is with us. "Be strong and courageous. Do not be afraid or terrified because of them, for the Lord your God goes with you; he will never leave you nor forsake you" (Deuteronomy 31:6).
- God is our helper. "So do not fear, for I am with you; do not be dismayed, for I am your God. I will strengthen you and help you; I will uphold you with my righteous right hand" (Isaiah 41:10).

And the Bible teaches us these two truths:

- God has a plan for your life. "For I know the plans I have for you," declares the Lord, "plans to prosper you and not to harm you, plans to give you hope and a future" (Jeremiah 29:11).
- And no one can thwart his plans. "For the Lord Almighty has purposed, and who can thwart him? His hand is stretched out, and who can turn it back?" (Isaiah 14:27).

Why can we trust God? The proof of God's goodness and his intentions for our good fill the pages of Scripture. It is because we know him that we know we can trust him.

Our ability to trust God more comes from our taking the time to know him better, to see his character not only in the pages of Scripture, but also in the workings of our lives.

A Battle Plan to Fight the Fear that We Can't Trust God

Still, in the day-to-day of life, we might find ourselves battling the fear that we can't trust God. When that happens, just as in all of our other fears, we need a battle plan.

1. Make the decision to trust daily

Our job is to decide to trust God every single day. The Holy Spirit's job is to give us the strength to do so. And God alone determines the outcome.

I love this so much. I just have to decide. The Holy Spirit does the work.

No matter what the day brings, make the decision to trust him.

I have a friend, Sarah, who practices this concept really well. She often tells me it's because she spent so much time trusting herself and her schemes, which got her nowhere. For example, some time ago her oldest son was in a terrible relationship. He had been dating a girl for several years, a girl the family loved, a girl my friend had led to Christ.

Over time, it became evident that the relationship was not what God had planned for either of their lives, but her son could not end it. According to my friend, it was torture watching them break up, then get back together, then break up, then get back together. So, she did what any good mom would do, she worried herself sick, then she came up with a plan that would get her son to stop thinking about this woman. She "arranged" for her son to "run into" the daughter of a friend at a church event. Long story short, that too ended in disaster, and her son nearly committed suicide over a second failed relationship. He deemed himself unlovable and seemed bent on proving just how unlovable he was.

She told me, "I learned two things during that time. One was that worrying didn't change a single thing. In fact, worrying is what led me to believe that I had to come up with a plan to 'fix things.' The second thing I learned was that when I finally accepted that I wasn't in control, nor should I be, I was able to release the anxiety and fear that came with the whole situation.

I told God, 'God, he's yours. This is yours. I know you have a plan. I'm just a part of his storm. And my job was probably to point him to you, but I didn't do that well. Please forgive me. And please take over!'"

She laughingly told me, "It was my 'Jesus take the wheel' moment! And trust me, I have not ever asked to drive again!" She knows from experience that trusting God is a way better plan.

I, like Sarah, have had to learn to make the decision to trust God every day.

Each day I pray these truths over myself and my family:

- *I surrender any illusion of control I have about today.*
- *I trust you, Lord, with my children. They are yours.*
- *I trust you, Lord, with my life and my future.*
- *I choose this day, and every day, to choose faith over fear.*
- *I choose to believe your promises are true.*
- *I choose to be comforted by your presence.*
- *I can't control the future, but I can choose to trust you.*

We may have to fight the battle on a daily basis, but we can win if we choose to do so.

You can say, *Today, Lord, I choose to trust you.* Then write out or pray exactly how you will choose to trust him.

2. Look for the progress

My friend said it all so well: "When we don't know how to trust God for ourselves, it is really important to look for him in the everyday details. He is faithful and cares about the little things that happen to us. When we learn to notice (and practice noticing) the places where he takes care of us in little everyday moments, we learn to trust him with the big things."

Our trust in God grows with practice. As we go through our lives, it's important to notice that we are making progress. This is really true of anything we do, but it's especially true of learning to trust. Recognizing we have trusted God in similar situations before makes it easier for us to trust him again. The more we have opportunity to trust, and the more we actually *do* trust, the easier trusting becomes. It's called making progress.

One great example of that from my own life is when my sons started school. With that first child, *man*, was it difficult to trust. I worried all day, every day, for most of his first year of school. Same was true of the second and third child. Finally, I realized, "I can't live my life in fear for my kids when they are out of my sight. I have to learn to entrust them to God." Now, each time I am tempted to worry about one of my boy's firsts (first day of school, first day of high school, first time driving, first date . . . you get the idea), I remember that I have entrusted them to God.

In many ways it's like the stones of remembrance I've talked about. Remembering God's faithfulness to us reminds us to trust in his goodness and his love for us, as well as his plan for our lives.

3. Trust his timing

We see in Genesis 12 that God promised Abraham that he would be the father to a great nation. At the time, Abraham was seventy-five years old and his wife, Sarah, was barren. I'm sure he and Sarah imagined that a child would come soon.

Then came Abraham's eightieth birthday. Still no child. Can you imagine how frustrated he was? Had he heard God right? Hadn't God promised him a child? Yes, God told him again, I'm still promising you "a son coming from your own body" (Genesis 15:4). So surely *now* God would act.

Nope.

Five more years ticked past. Five more years of childlessness and barrenness and pain. Finally, Sarah decided to take things into her own hands. "The Lord has kept me from having children," she pointed out to her husband. "Go, sleep with my maidservant; perhaps I can build a family through her" (Genesis 16:2).

And that's when Abraham messed up royally. Instead of hanging on to the promise of God, he had a child with his servant, Hagar.

At eighty-six years old Abraham had a son, Ishmael, but Sarah was still childless. Hagar made sure she remembered that regularly, and Sarah was beside herself with grief and envy. Sure, Abraham seemed happy because he now had a son, but what about *her*? So when an angel of the Lord came to her at age eighty-nine and told her that *she* would bear a son at age ninety, she laughed!

But then, just as God had first promised twenty-five years earlier, in God's perfect timing, Abraham and Sarah had a son together. Abraham was one hundred. Sarah was ninety. Their son Isaac was a true miracle. But instead of anticipating the miracle, they experienced much self-created heartache.

God had been building Abraham and Sarah's faith bit by bit over time. Just imagine if they had only trusted God and waited for his timing. Sarah and Abraham could have spent those years joyfully awaiting the fulfillment of God's promise. Instead they spent them embroiled in jealousy and heartache.

Admittedly, trusting in God's perfect timing is a lesson I have always wanted to skip over. I'm like Veruca Salt from *Charlie and the Chocolate Factory*: "Don't ask how, I want it now!" And you know how God *teaches* you to wait for his perfect timing? He makes you *wait* for his perfect timing.

I've heard many people say, "God is never early, and he's never late. He's always right on time." God has perfect timing. I know that. But I'm not great at waiting, so it's a lesson he will probably be teaching me over and over until I'm ninety.

4. Stay mindful of who is trying to steal your trust and peace

My favorite T-shirt is a simple heather gray one with big, white, block letters that spell out "Not Today, Satan." We don't want to stay constantly focused on our enemy and blame everything on him (our dying iPhone battery or the fact that our dog ate our favorite shoes probably aren't examples of spiritual attacks), but it doesn't do us any favors to forget who our enemy is and how he tries to derail us. When the feelings of fear, worry, and anxiety start to flow in, I love to put on that shirt and say out loud, "Not today, Satan. God has *not* given me a spirit of fear; but of power, and of love, and of a sound mind."

There's nothing like starting the day with a light-hearted reminder that we are in a battle, but we are great women of God and aren't to be messed with. Sometimes that is done with something as simple as wearing a funny T-shirt.

5. Sing an anthem or song of gratitude

In the Bible there are 185 songs. Songs of happiness, battle songs, songs of grief, songs sung in fear. Even entire books of the Bible are songs, including Psalms, Lamentations (kind of like the blues of the Bible), and Song of Songs.

This is not by accident. The Bible is filled with music because music speaks to our souls. When David was deliriously happy, he danced and sang. When he was overcome with grief, he sang. For every season in life, whether in joy or sorrow, he sang praises to his Father in heaven, and through that praise he found peace.

In our day-to-day lives, it's important to work in rituals of worship and praise. There's no better way to combat the enemy's attacks and keep yourself focused on trusting God than with music.

Recently I've fallen in love with the classic hymn "Great Is Thy Faithfulness." I sing it with passion around my house so loud that I occasionally scare Mollie, and she ends up hiding behind the couch.

Great is thy faithfulness, O God my Father,
There is no shadow of turning with thee;
Thou changest not, thy compassions, they fail not
As thou hast been thou forever wilt be.

Great is thy faithfulness! Great is thy faithfulness!
Morning by morning new mercies I see;
All I have needed thy hand hath provided—
Great is thy faithfulness, Lord, unto me!

We choose to worship and praise so the fear and anxieties of the day don't swallow us up. In our praise we proclaim out loud over our lives that we are never alone, that we serve a God who loves us completely, and that his plans for us are good.

Whether you are walking through a storm right now or you see storm clouds looming on the horizon, take comfort in the fact that God will never leave you. God is a good Father who goes before you, stands behind you, and walks beside you. We serve a good God who loves us and is worthy of our trust.

Great is thy faithfulness, Lord, unto me!

Action Steps

Go to page 219 for a list of truth declarations that you can speak over your life daily.

- Have you experienced viewing God through the lens of your earthly father? What does that feel like to you?
- Check out my playlist of favorite worship songs for any situation you are going through at AlliWorthington.com/Playlists.

BRAVE AND UNAFRAID

Almost four years have passed since Mark's struggle with asthma began, but Mark hasn't yet been miraculously healed. In fact, even as I'm typing these words to you today, he is struggling. Still, we are praying, hoping, and believing that one day here on earth he will be healed. In the meantime, though, Mark and I have declared that we aren't going to let the enemy use this situation to destroy us. Instead, we cling to the truth that God is good; he does good in our lives; and he will give us the strength to come out on the other side victorious.

In this we know that we are no longer slaves to fear, but we can find peace, strength, and courage in him. We are children of the most high; we are more than conquerors in Christ (Romans 8:37); we are part of a royal priesthood (1 Peter 2:9); and no weapon formed against us will prosper (Isaiah 54:17).

> His perfect love casts out fear when we cast our fearful hearts on him.

Remaining a slave to fear is remaining tormented by the enemy. It's not how we were created to live. Jesus didn't die on the cross to save our souls from hell so we would live here on earth riddled with anxiety, worries, and fears. He gave us a helper, the Holy Spirit, to give us courage, strength, and power.

There comes a time when we have to decide to believe all the things he tells us about himself, to believe what he tells us about ourselves, to stand up strong and tall and pronounce, *I am a child of God.* Because of these truths, because of this freedom, we will fight and we will win the battle in the war he has already won.

Fear, anxiety, and worry will no longer hold us down.

When I was a little girl, my mom would pray over me every night. She prayed that I would grow to be a great woman of God, strong in my faith, and fearless as I faced the future.

And that, my friend, is my prayer for you—that you continue to walk this journey with strength and courage. Because you are a great woman of God, strong in your faith, and fearless in the face of the future.

We have Jesus; we have the power of the Holy Spirit in us; we can replace lies with truth; and we have our battle plan. We are no longer slaves to fear; we're fearless children of God.

In this world we will have trouble, yet we know who overcomes the world. We know we can trust him to take care of us. Yes, the storms will come, but we don't have to be beaten on the rocks of the shore. We can weather the storm even when the waves roll higher than the edges of our lives. And no matter what storms roll in, we know he is always with us; his promise and his presence are there.

We don't have to live in fear. God is in control; he has only goodness and hope for our future; and we can trust him as a good Father.

Over this past year there've been so many women who, when they learn I'm writing a book about fear, lean in close and whisper, "Alli, that book is for me." They tell me stories of the fear and worry and anxieties that have them hiding under the covers, feeling like they're about to drown, and wondering if Jesus is asleep when they need him most.

When that happens, I lean in even closer, grab their hands in mine, and with an intensity that takes people by surprise I whisper, "Get on your face and talk to Jesus. Ask for a fresh filling of the Holy Spirit. Worship him even when the storm rages around you. Then stand up tall and go fight the enemy."

And that's your commissioning in this book. Get on your face, talk to Jesus, pour out everything in your heart so you can be healed, and ask the Holy Spirit (who is given to us by Jesus as our helper and comforter) to empower you to do everything that you're called to do in this season. Worship God when the storm clouds appear on the horizon and when the cold wind whips across your face, and *use this battle plan to fight back.*

The verse that I pray you will write across your life is Proverbs 31:25, "She is clothed with strength and dignity; she can laugh at the days to come."

Stay strong. Stay close to Jesus. Find courageous battle buddies and lock arms and hearts and join the fight. Stand tall, great woman of God, you are clothed with strength and dignity, and you can laugh bravely at the days to come.

That's the secret; that's how we live brave and unafraid.

That's how this scared girl learned to fight.

YOUR
BATTLE
PLAN

I grew up watching those old war movies with my granddaddy. (They were just so terrible and so great at the same time!) My favorite part was always when the generals rolled out their big battle plans and talked about how they were going to win the war. I could just imagine the maps and the drawings and the secret plans written out on those pieces of paper.

Friend, these are your battle plans. Hands-on tools you can use as you are fighting your fears, wrestling your worries, and overcoming your anxieties. I can just imagine the great plans you will write on these pages! But remember that the tools only work if you pick them up and use them. Use them to be encouraged when the battle is hard, to help you when you get stuck, to process the things that feel hard, and to keep yourself one step ahead of the enemy. You've got this!

Download your custom battle plan today:
AlliWorthington.com/BattlePlan

The Five Bad B's

Busy

Blame

Bury

Binge

Brood

Go to
AlliWorthington.com/FiveBadBs
for your printable copy.

The Four Good A's

Aware

Be aware of your feelings.

Avoid the Five B's

Don't numb your feelings.

Ask Jesus for help

Take it to Jesus and let him fight the spiritual battle.

Attack

Practice the battle plan to take care of
anxieties on the physical plane.

―――――

Go to
AlliWorthington.com/FourGoodAs
for your printable copy.

Truth Talk Exercise

Use these next two pages for some truth talk. Write down your unhealthy thoughts and worries and replace them with a statement of truth. It's a great way to fight back against fear!

Example:

Unhealthy Thoughts

Things will never get better. I am a failure;
there's no reason even to try.

Healthy Thoughts

I know the spirit of the risen Christ lives in me
and will empower me to do all I need to do.
I am not a failure; I am a child of God.

Unhealthy Thoughts

_____

_____

_____

Healthy Thoughts

_____

_____

_____

209

Unhealthy Thoughts

_____

_____

_____

Healthy Thoughts

_____

_____

_____

Unhealthy Thoughts

_____

_____

_____

Healthy Thoughts

_____

_____

_____

Don't Quit: Personalized Bible Verses

To fight back against fear, speak these personalized Bible verses over yourself and your situation. Write or speak your name in the blank spaces.

"God has not given me, _____, the spirit of fear; but of power, and of love, and of a sound mind" (2 Timothy 1:7 NKJV).

"I, _____, have been brought to fullness in Christ. He is the head over every power and authority" (Colossians 2:10).

"I, _____, have the peace of God, which transcends all understanding, and it will guard my heart and my mind in Christ Jesus" (Philippians 4:7).

"It is for freedom that Christ has set me free. I, ___, will stand firm and not be burdened again by the yoke of slavery" (Galatians 5:1).

"I, _____, am God's handiwork, created in Christ Jesus to do good things, which God prepared in advance for me to do" (Ephesians 2:10).

"God began a good work in me, _____, and he will

carry it on to completion until the day of Christ Jesus" (Philippians 1:6).

"God makes me, _____, stand firm in Christ. He anointed me, set his seal of ownership on me, and put his Spirit in my heart as a deposit, guaranteeing what is to come" (2 Corinthians 1:21–22).

"And God will meet all my needs according to the riches of his glory in Christ Jesus" (Philippians 4:19).

"Neither height nor depth, nor anything else in all creation, will be able to separate _____ from the love that is in Christ Jesus" (Romans 8:39).

"Because of Jesus, _____ is free from all condemnation" (Romans 8:1).

Reframing Our Thoughts

Identify a current negative thought pattern you are battling. Now reframe your thoughts in a positive way. Write down the reframed thought and refer to it every time that negative thought resurfaces.

Example:

Unhealthy Thoughts

All my friends have more fun than I do.
Why does my life have to be so hard?

Healthy Thoughts

It may look like it on Instagram, but everyone has their ups and downs. I know God has plans for good for me, and even when my today is hard, I can look forward to my tomorrow.

Unhealthy Thoughts

_____

_____

_____

Healthy Thoughts

_____

_____

_____

Unhealthy Thoughts

_____

_____

_____

Healthy Thoughts

_____

_____

_____

———— ~~ ————

Unhealthy Thoughts

_____

_____

_____

Healthy Thoughts

_____

_____

_____

———— ~~ ————

Reframing your thoughts takes
the power away from the enemy and
allows you to regain your peace.

Right-Thinking Practice

Think about a certain worry or fear you have and take it through the "right-thinking test."

1. How likely is this to happen?

_____

_____

_____

_____

_____

2. Is there any evidence this is a risk?

_____

_____

_____

_____

_____

3. Even if this is a risk, how much control do I actually have over the situation?

_____

_____

_____

_____

_____

Identifying the Lies of the Enemy

As we uncovered in the "What If I Never Measure Up?" chapter, the enemy speaks lies over us and tries to stop us from living the life we are created to live. Take a few moments to pray and ask God to reveal to you what lies you have believed, and then replace them with truth.

The Screwtape Letters Game

Take a situation you are facing right now and ask yourself: "If I were the enemy, what three things would I say to derail me?"

First Way:

_____

_____

_____

_____

_____

_____

Second Way:

_____

_____

_____

_____

_____

Third Way:

_____

_____

_____

_____

_____

Are You Too Hard on Yourself?

Ask yourself the five questions to determine if you are too hard on yourself. Circle the answer that fits most of the time. Don't overthink it.

1. Do you feel guilty when you relax?

   Yes   No   Sometimes

2. Do you talk to yourself in a way you wouldn't talk to others?

   Yes   No   Sometimes

3. Do you expect perfection from yourself?

   Yes   No   Sometimes

4. Do you suffer from imposter syndrome?

   Yes   No   Sometimes

5. Do you beat yourself up over things that are out of your control?

   Yes   No   Sometimes

If you answered two or more with *yes*, or three or more with *sometimes*, it's time to give yourself less criticism and more compassion.

Truths to Speak Over Your Life Every Day

I SURRENDER ANY ILLUSION OF
CONTROL I HAVE ABOUT TODAY.

———

I TRUST YOU, LORD, WITH MY
CHILDREN. THEY ARE YOURS.

———

I TRUST YOU, LORD, WITH MY
LIFE AND MY FUTURE.

———

TODAY AND EVERY DAY, I CHOOSE
FAITH OVER FEAR.

———

I CHOOSE TO BELIEVE YOUR
PROMISES ARE TRUE.

———

I CHOOSE TO BE COMFORTED
BY YOUR PRESENCE.

———

I CAN'T CONTROL THE FUTURE, BUT
I CAN CHOOSE TO TRUST YOU.

Go to
AlliWorthington.com/LifeTruths
for your printable copy.

_____ is clothed with

strength

and

dignity;

_____ can laugh

at the days to come.

PROVERBS 31:25

ACKNOWLEDGMENTS

My Family—

Thank you, Mark, for allowing me to share our struggles, our love and our stories with the world. Your support of me, my calling, and my crazy ideas through the years means the world to me. Justin, this year you are off to college and I'm so proud of the man you have become. Set your face against the wind and stand firm. Jack, Joey, James, and Jeremiah—Thank you for the patience as I hid away in my office writing on the weekends. You guys make me so happy every day. I love you and you make being your mom such a joy. Jessica and Andy, you are both so strong and loving. I am so proud of you both and your marriage. I love you so much!

My Colleagues—

Thank you to my agent, Jenni Burke, for the constant support and wise sounding board. Sandy Vander Zicht, I have so much love and admiration for you and your work. Years ago you saw the beautiful symphony in the middle of a mess of sounds and I'm so thankful to be able to follow your lead. Alicia Kasen, you make dreaming up new ways to share my heart fun again. Thank you for stepping in and seeing the forest when I'm lost in the trees.

My Encouragers—

Carol Jones, thank you for helping me make sense of all the ideas on my heart and find a way to express them clearly. Megan Jordan, thank you for the hours of truth talk and laughter. Bianca Olthoff, thank you for stirring up courage in me to step into the promised land.

NOTES

Chapter 2: The Five Bad B's

1. Alli Worthingon, *Breaking Busy* (Grand Rapids, Mich.: Zondervan, 2015), 113.
2. Monita Karmakar and Jessica Sloan Kruger, "Is Binge-Watching Bad for Your Mental Health?" *The Guardian*, March 4, 2016, http://www.theguardian.com/commentisfree/2016/mar/04/binge-watching-mental-health-effects-research.

Chapter 4: What If They Don't Like Me?

1. Guy Winch, *Emotional First Aid: Healing Rejection, Guilt, Failure, and Other Everyday Hurts* (New York: Hudson Street Press, 2013), 4.
2. Morrison, Deborah, and Arvindh Singh. "Overgeneralization: Cognitive Distortions Depression." NEXUS. February 09, 2008. Accessed February 25, 2017. https://nexusnovel.wordpress.com/2006/08/30/overgeneralization-cognitive-distortions-depression/.
3. Weir, Kristen. "The Pain of Social Rejection." Pardon Our Interruption. April 2012. Accessed February 25, 2017. http://www.apa.org/monitor/2012/04/rejection.aspx.

Chapter 6: What If I Can't Do This?

1. Brennan Manning, *Ruthless Trust: The Ragamuffin's Path to God* (New York: HarperCollins, 2000), 15.

Chapter 8: What If Everyone Has Fun without Me?

1. https://www.researchgate.net/publication/236260708_
Motivational_Emotional_and_Behavioral_Correlates_of_Fear_
of_Missing_Out Accessed 8.27.16.
2. http://www.abc.net.au/news/2015–11–08/wellbeing-survey-finds
-teens-feeling-left-out-on-social-media/6921780. Accessed 8.27.16.

Chapter 10: What If I Never Measure Up?

1. "Maya Angelou: The Lessons & The Legacy." OutWrite Living
with Starla J. King. May 28, 2014. Accessed February 25, 2017.
http://outwriteliving.com/maya-angelou-the-lessons-the-legacy/.

STAY CONNECTED WITH ALLI

Hi, new friend. I'm honored that you are on this fierce faith adventure, too! I have prayed for you and your journey moving from fear to fierce faith. I would love to stay connected with you on social media and with my Friday Devotionals. You'll receive a short, encouraging note from me every Friday morning. Let's continue on this journey together!

Online:
AlliWorthington.com

Instagram:
@AlliWorthington

Friday Devotionals:
Alliworthington.com/Friday-Devotionals